Managing Your
Human Resources

Managing Your Human Resources

A Partnership Approach

LOUIS V. IMUNDO
and
MARTIN P. EISERT

amacom

American Management Associations

To my sons—Lou, Larry, and Danny—each of whom
in his own way has enriched my life.

L. V. Imundo

To my Creator, who gave me intelligence, and to my wife,
Kathy, who encouraged me to use it.

M. P. Eisert

Library of Congress Cataloging in Publication Data

Imundo, Louis V.
  Managing your human resources.

  Includes index.
  1. Personnel management.   I. Eisert, Martin P.
II. Title.
HF5549.I49   658.3   82-71305
ISBN 0-8144-5708-8   AACR2

First Printing

Preface

Over the past 20 years we have witnessed many changes in our society, in its organizations, and in the people who live and work in it. In particular, within organizations we have observed the expanding scope of activities and influence of the personnel function, or what is currently identified as the human resources function. Many factors have contributed to this expansion, which has significantly affected the ways managers manage and organizations function.

One would expect managers in all organizational functions and at all levels to openly embrace the expanding role of the human resources function, but as that role changed, it became apparent that personnel specialists were frequently unwelcomed by managers. Either tacit acceptance or covert or even overt resistance to human resources specialists was the norm rather than the exception. Our observations as a consultant and human resources executive led us to examine the reasons for this situation.

We concluded that the major cause underlying the conflict between human resources specialists and managers was essentially misunderstanding on both sides. We reasoned that if the misunderstandings could be resolved, the groundwork would exist for increasing managers' effectiveness and efficiency, as well as for building more cooperative working relationships between management and employees.

This thought became the central theme for the book. We knew that many works on personnel management, industrial relations, and human resources management had already been published. Nearly all of them follow the same track—they are directed at people working in the human resources profession or people studying to enter it. Only in an indirect way are they directed toward managers.

This book, then, is not a traditional book on human resources management. It is aimed primarily at managers and only indirectly at human resources specialists. Our objective is to show managers in all kinds and sizes of organizations and at all levels how to utilize the human resources function and its specialists more effectively.

As usual, the authors' debts exceed the number that can reasonably be acknowledged in a prefatory note, but we especially want to thank F. W. Hirt, President, Erie Insurance Group, and T. B. Hagen, Executive Vice-President, for their support and encouragement of this project; and Father Tom Kelley, rector of St. Mark's Seminary, who unselfishly provided a quiet haven to think and write. It goes without saying that any shortcomings in this book are solely our responsibility.

Louis V. Imundo

Martin P. Eisert

Contents

1

Understanding Organizations, Environments, and the Human Resources Function

The far-reaching changes we have witnessed over the past few decades have significantly, and at times dramatically, affected the way people think and act. The impact of the sudden and rapid increase in the price of oil and oil-based products, starting in the 1970s and continuing today, is a recent example of how radically events can change people's lives in a short span of time. The most basic objective of any society, organization, or individual is to survive for the duration of a desired or planned existence. Some organizations, such as a business corporation, will strive to exist indefinitely, while others, such as an election campaign committee, have a preplanned end to its existence.

Genetic programming, environmentally caused deterioration, accidents, and the fact that medical technology has not progressed to the point where all the major human organs can be replaced as they wear out, limit most people to a preplanned life span of less than a hundred years. However, through reproduction, part of a person can, in a sense, continue to live on, even though the individual has expired. Societies and organizations can theoretically survive much longer than one person because they can replenish or replace with substitutes much of what wears out, including their human resources. Survival, however, is related not only to replacing what wears out, but also to the ability to respond and adapt to changes in the environment. The term "environment" refers to any economic, legal, political, psychological, or social, as well as natural or physical factor that can or actually does affect something's ability to function. And unless an organization is able to maintain its existence through some form of direct or indirect control over its environment, its survival is ultimately determined by the ability to adapt to environmental changes. In any environment where change occurs continuously, only those who are able to respond effectively and adapt will continue to survive.

The Responsibility of Managing

In highly competitive environments with continual change occuring, management is a "survival of the fittest" profession, one that is physically, emotionally, and intellectually challenging. Managers, especially those whose decisions impact heavily on the way an organization functions, must remain continually alert to the need to change. The organization as well as the individual who cannot or will not adapt to external events when necessary will face likely diminishment of power and eventual demise.

Managers as Trustees

Business organizations exist essentially to serve the needs of others. Business organizations, especially those operating on a profit-making basis in competitive environments, must remain sensitive to the changing needs of those they specifically serve, their employees, and society as a whole, all of whom, in different ways, sanction their existence and allow them to function. To varying degrees, in the short term, an organization may exert more influence or direct control over its environment (that is, society, customers, employees, and others) than the elements in that environment, individually or collectively, exert on it. However, in the long term, even for the largest and most powerful organizations, the balance of power tilts in favor of society. Many an organization has had its power curtailed by forces of the marketplace, government legislation, unionization, and precedent-setting legal actions brought on by an individual or a group.

Human beings are territorial creatures, often going to great lengths to stake out and protect their territory and, when the opportunity presents itself, to expand it. Having a job title and accompanying position is a form of territorializing. What people who own and/or manage organizations often fail to recognize, or if they do recognize it, fail to accept, is the fact that they are trustees. For example, possession of an organization's stock certificates or some other title of ownership continues only as long as society sanctions it. American corporations with facilities in foreign countries have found that titles of ownership are worthless when foreign governments decide that it is not in their peoples' best interests to sanction private ownership.

Managers may have varying organizational titles bestowed on them, but they do not own their jobs: They are trustees of responsibilities inherent in positions. To meet their responsibilities, they must acquire and use power. Legitimatized power is commonly referred to as authority. Management must use its authority in ways that are perceived to be acceptable to the environment. There are no inherent prerogatives. Ultimately, power that is abused or misused will be curtailed or removed.

Society and people, whether or not they are fully cognizant of it, place great faith in organizations and the people who manage them. People expect the lights to go on when they flick the switch. They expect the telephone to work when they lift the receiver. The more people expect from organizations, the more faith they put in them. As a result, the responsibilities of organizations and those who manage them increase in proportion to the rise in society's expectations. Managers must understand, however, that their individual responsibilities will always exceed their authority. Because societies and individuals tend to be perpetually wanting, they place never-ending demands on organizations and their managers. Whether or not managers like this arrangement is really irrelevant.

Organizations, and in particular large organizations, have a responsibility to function effectively and efficiently for the period of their desired or intended existence. In allowing organizations to exist, society also allows them to use or consume scarce and often nonreplenishable resources. When organizations provide more products and services than they consume in human and material resources, their existence is an asset. When organizations whose products or services are either desired or essential fail prematurely, they have consumed more than they have provided and their existence was more of a liability than an asset to the environment.

Adapting to Change

The events of the past few decades have complicated our world. In terms of interrelationships and interdependencies, this is true of both societies and organizations. At the same time, the world has become a place of many new opportunities and challenges. Our delayed recognition and acceptance of the scarcity of many natural resources, for which we have often been unable to develop economic substitutes, have dramatically and significantly altered our life-styles and thinking. The problems caused by scarcity have also created opportunities and challenges to provide solutions for them. Whether they exist for profit or not, organizations that can avoid devastating problems while capitalizing on opportunities and meeting challenges will be the ones that survive and prosper. Organizations that greatly influence our lives today may no longer exist in 20 years, and ones that do not even exist today may become the household words of tomorrow.

Changes are inevitable and will continue to occur whether we like it or not. Indeed, we live in a period of accelerated change. Change is a force that continually attempts to throw us off balance. Organizations and individuals are constantly engaged in trying to maintain themselves in a state of dynamic equilibrium. The product of instability or disequilibrium is an action to move toward stability or equilibrium. Organizations and their managements, whether they effect change or are affected by it, must eventually respond to it in order to regain a balance with the environment. Change per se is neither good nor bad. How it is perceived, how it is acted on or reacted to, and ultimately what results are derived from it determine whether it is good or bad.

Growth and Bureaucracy

Both organizations and individuals are creatures of habit. Some are flexible and adaptive to change, while others are not. As organizations grow, they tend to move toward disorder, which can lead to loss of control. Inconsistency, inefficiency, and loss of control then motivate managers to either maintain centralized personal control or develop centralized, depersonalized control in the form of policies, procedures, and practices. Controls, whether personalized through an individual or depersonalized through a policy or procedure, bring about consistency and order. Since controls place restrictions on individual choices of behavior, however, they are not always welcomed by those who value individuality and independence. Fortunately, though, people also dislike instability, and when it reaches an unacceptable level they will welcome controls.

Once executive-level managers make the policy decisions to implement controls, others are usually left the task of developing additional procedural mechanisms to ensure compliance with them. Over time, whether or not they agree with the controls, the majority of the organization's members will adjust their behavior to them and will function within the organization's defined limits of what is considered acceptable. Naturally, the more disagreement that exists on the fairness of such limits or constraints, the higher the probability of overt or covert resistance to them. If

the constraints are viewed as reasonable and are fairly administered, acceptance will usually become ingrained. As environments and people change, however, perceptions of the reason-
ableness of constraints on behavior often change as well. This
frequently leads to conflict.

As policies are created by executive-level managers and procedures are subsequently written to make them operational, others
at lower organizational levels are assigned the responsibility for
ensuring consistent compliance. Some members, because of their
unique training and experience, are given the responsibility of
recommending policies to executive-level managers. As an organization grows, the number of policies and procedures tends to
increase proportionally. All too frequently, those charged with
administering policies and procedures lose sight of their intended
role and assume that to justify their continued existence they
need to create more procedures and recommend even more
policies. Additional policies and procedures, in turn, generate a
need for more people to administer them. If this bureaucratiza-
tion continues unchecked, slow paralysis of the organization results.

The more complacent an organization becomes about its own
bureaucracy, the less responsive it wants to be or is capable of
being to external and internal forces of change. People, like organizations, can also become bureaucratized and inflexible. Competent managers, especially those who manage in organizations
where the need to change arises frequently, recognize when bu-
reaucratization is occurring and take steps to terminate the process before it does too much damage.

Evolution of the Personnel Function

The process of managing is not a recent phenomenon, as some
notable writers would have us believe. Nor is personnel, or what
we now call human resources management. The management of

people always has been and will continue to be a basic part of the management process, implicit in every manager's role. When societies and organizations were smaller and less complex, the management of people was simpler. As the rate of growth and change in societies, organizations, and technology increased, so did changes in people's values, expectations, and attitudes. As a result, organizations and managers often found themselves unable to function as effectively as they needed or wanted to.

Historically, business organizations have placed greater emphasis on the production of products and services than on concern for the welfare of employees. Considerable criticism is still directed at managers who have become notorious because of their aggressive pursuit of productivity and profits. Were these people as malicious as many commentators would have us believe, or did they function in a way that was accepted and considered normal during their lifetimes? Many, because of their power and what they perceived as control over their environment, did resist modifying their behavior even though the signals for change were strong. The rest is history. Change was eventually forced on those organizations and their leaders. Only truly well-managed organizations and far-seeing managers recognized the need to show more concern for the welfare of employees before they were compelled to do so by the forces of change emanating from the environment.

Although managers claim that employees are an organization's most valuable resource, their actions frequently demonstrate otherwise. Concern for the well-being of employees tends to be abandoned as businesses pursue production and profits, especially when the organization's survival is at stake. From a historical perspective, management's long-standing lack of concern for the well-being of employees prompted the rise and growth of unions and protective employee and social welfare laws. Precedent-setting decisions of courts and government administrative agencies followed. To a degree, these actions influenced the birth and development of the specialized personnel function. Some organizations created personnel departments out of genuine concern for the welfare of employees. Most did so in reaction to forces pressing for change. Unfortunately, many managers react to hindsight as opposed to acting with foresight.

The Personnel Function as a Response to Complexity

As mentioned, unions, enacted legislation, and, at times, vigorous application of the law by courts and government administrative agencies influenced the growth and development of the specialized personnel function. However, there were other factors.

The growth of organizations, both in number of employees and complexity of structure, led to increased specialization in general and with it the development of the personnel function. The twentieth century has been a period of greater and greater specialization. As organizations have grown, so has their need for specialists. Even a small organization, which usually cannot afford the luxury of employing specialists on its staff, will have to buy skills and knowledge on an ad hoc basis, especially if the skills needed are not directly related to daily operation. Countless numbers of organizations have sprung up out of nowhere to furnish specialized services to those who do not keep specialists on their staffs. A problem, however, with specialists in any field is that they tend to develop tunnel vision. Often they understand their own roles but fail to grasp the roles of others and how they all must interface. Differences in role perceptions between operations-oriented specialists and support- or service-oriented specialists cause unavoidable conflicts.

Attracting and Retaining Personnel

The development of the personnel function was also influenced by the needs of organizations to attract and select the appropriate people for specialized positions. In the past, these tasks were easily accomplished. These are some of the factors that now make attraction and selection of candidates more difficult and call for the skills of specialists:

- Changes in technology creating supply-and-demand imbalances between jobs and qualified candidates.
- Scarcity of people to fill many unskilled positions because the welfare system suppresses incentives to work.
- Layer upon layer of confusing and often contradictory government regulations that affect all facets of the employment process.
- Where unions are present, restrictions on management's flexibility and authority as stipulated in the negotiated labor agreement.
- Scarcity of available labor caused by rapid organizational growth.

The need to properly utilize and retain the better employees also gave impetus to the growth of the personnel function. In the past, spending an entire working career with one or two employers was the norm rather than the exception for most employees. Today, this is not so. Given the fact that hiring people is an expensive process, when good employees leave prematurely, the loss is costly. Because of the following factors, increasingly specialized employee-relations skills were needed in this area as well:

High mobility of people, giving them the flexibility to relocate when they decide to change employers.

Changing values and attitudes about loyalty, responsibility, authority, compensation, and commitment.

Influence of unions and threats of unionization and government legislation.

Competition among employers for each other's employees.

Change in management's attitudes about employees.

Changing technology and the need to train or retrain employees for newly created jobs.

Availability of trained people to fill positions created by growth.

Need to maintain a competitive compensation program.

Need to protect the physical and mental health of employees because of the high costs incurred when their health fails.

The Importance of Management's Attitude

The entire scope of responsibility of the personnel function centers on two key activities. They are "employment" and "employee relations." Essentially, employment activities pertain to the organization's people, that is, its employees. Employee-relations activities focus on the operational environment in which employees have to function. The role of the personnel function in an organization is often a reflection of this environment, which is by and large determined by executive-level management's attitude, both toward its employees and toward the personnel function. On the one hand, human resources can be viewed on the same level of importance as production, finance, and marketing; on the other hand, it may be seen as a necessary, but unwanted, function whose influence should be kept to a minimum. Nearly everyone accepts the fact that neglect and abuse of employees has given way to policies that reflect concern. The question is, to what extent have managers' attitudes really changed? In most organizations, is the personnel function considered as important as production, finance, and marketing, or is it still relegated to a paper-shuffling role?

The concern-for-employees movement started many decades ago. Some people will argue that managers have become overly concerned, while others will argue the opposite. This country has recently passed through a lengthy period of liberalism, starting in the 1930s and terminating, at least for now, at the end of the 1970s.

For a variety of reasons, this nation's productivity has declined. In fact, in many industries the situation is serious. With little doubt, management's concern for productivity and profitability will increase. Managers, throughout the 1980s and beyond, will have to strike a delicate balance between concern for the welfare and development of employees and the need to compete effectively in the marketplace. Will the increasing emphasis on production and profits be at the expense of interest in people's welfare? In our opinion, some decrease in concern for employees will have to occur. It will not be a significant decrease, because too many safeguards that have been built into the social framework would have to fail before any radical change could take place. If managements learn to utilize their human resources more effectively at all organizational levels, then the goals of increased productivity and profitability without sacrificing the welfare of employees could be achieved. Making this statement, however, is far easier than accomplishing it.

Achieving this goal will require the highest possible level of skills and teamwork. Barriers to cooperation will have to be reduced to allow greater productivity without substantial increase in costs. The price paid for failure by society, organizations, and people will be high.

Emergence of the Human Resources Function

Many people are unfamiliar with the term "human resources." Most readers still think of the human resources function as "personnel" or "industrial relations." It is only within the last few years that many organizations have changed the name "personnel" to "human resources." Is the name change a form of window dressing in an effort to stay in style, or does it have a deeper meaning? In some organizations it is nothing more than a name change. In others, it represents a recognition that the function's role in the organization is different.

Personnel as a specialized organizational function is, for the most part, a twentieth-century phenomenon. It was created by and has grown out of external and internal forces of change. Historically, it has been concerned with the processing of paperwork. It has had little if any influence on important decisions about employees. Over the past few decades and especially during the 1960s and 1970s, its role and influence have been considerably expanded.

As the scope of activities of personnel increased, its title changed. The term "human resources" emerged from a recognition by many managers that employees are indeed an organization's most important asset. An implicit part of the personnel function's responsibility is to help management protect, as well as make the best use of its human resources. Enlightened managers are aware that the human resources specialists can help them achieve the goals of productivity and profitability without misusing or burning out employees. Enlightened human resources specialists recognize that in performing its functions, management must strike a balance in serving its customers, society at large, and its employees.

The Scope of the Human Resources Function

From its roots as a paperwork-processing activity staffed by people with limited skills and managed by someone whom the organization had nowhere else to put without harming itself, human resources has evolved into a sophisticated profession employing highly capable people with considerable education and experience. The function's primary responsibilities still center on employment and employee relations. However, for all the reasons stated previously, many specialized activities have emerged from these two primary responsibilities. The following list covers typical activities:

Affirmative action	Incentive systems
Communications	Job analysis
Counseling	Job design
Education and training	Job evaluation
Employee health	Labor agreement
Exit interviewing	administration
Grievance handling	Negotiations
Health and welfare benefits	Orientation

Performance appraisal   Retirement
Performance standards   Safety and security
Personnel planning   Salary administration
Recruitment   Selection interviews
Rehabilitation   Testing
Relocation   Transfer and promotion

The larger the organization, the broader the scope of activities of the human resources function. In this age of specialization, as functional activities multiply and become more narrowly defined, the number of people staffiing these positions increases. These specialists all too often also possess narrowly defined training. Unfortunately, specialization can lead to this kind of diminished perspective, and often people may understand their own jobs well but have little or no idea how what they do fits into the organization's overall operations. The human resources function is in a uniquely sensitive position because its activities impinge on the entire organization; the larger its scope of activities, the greater its impact.

Understanding the Sources of Conflict

The increase in size and influence of the human resources function over the organization has not always been welcomed by management. It is not unusual to see managers and some support groups use their power to restrict this expansion. When people live and work together, disagreement or conflict is inevitable and unavoidable because of differing values, attitudes, and perceptions, scarcity of things people want, competitiveness, and ego factors. Conflict per se is not bad. In fact, if channeled properly, it can be constructive. But if allowed to go uncontrolled, it can be highly destructive. Conflict between human resources and other functions is often more frequent and intense than among other organizational units.

Territoriality and the Power Issue

To control conflict and channel it toward constructive outcomes, it is necessary to discover its sources. As mentioned earlier, human beings are territorial and, as such, compete for control of territory. In large measure, the history of the world can be reduced to struggles to acquire and retain territory. Within an organization, territory can be loosely defined as space occupied or controlled; numbers and types of people controlled; size of budget; and influence over decisions. It essentially boils down to control over the environment. If sufficient amounts of all the things people want were readily and continuously available, there would be less likelihood of conflict. In reality, we live in a world of scarcity. The greater the degree of scarcity, the more intense the competition will be for what is available.

One of the attractions of being a manager is the right to acquire, retain, and use power. Once power has been obtained and its benefits enjoyed, most people will not give it away or share it. Many factors affect people's needs to acquire power and their desire or willingness to share or dispense it. Managers frequently compete for power, in part because the right to use power is a tremendous source of ego satisfaction. It can be argued that most managers decentralize authority only out of necessity. Organizations continually struggle with the growth-versus-control dilemma. Growing too fast or too large can result in a loss of control. Overcontrol, on the other hand, often imposed because of a fear of losing control, can paralyze the organization's capacity to grow and take advantage of opportunities.

The Human Resources Function Seen as a Threat

In some organizations, the political battles for control of territory and, in effect, of the internal environment, can be ongoing and intense. Continued, intense battling consumes considerable resources and weakens the organization. If fighting and dissension are allowed to continue unchecked, an organization can conceivably destroy itself. Most organizations and their managers, however, do not consume themselves in the fires of conflict. Either a strong centralized authority controls the organization and thus controls the frequency and intensity of territorial conflicts, or the stronger managers who respect and fear one another negotiate truces. In most if not all organizations, tacit agreements among managers exist stipulating nonencroachment on one another's territory. Territorial boundaries and agreements to protect them are carefully shaped by these tacit understandings and prescribed rituals for operating. Occasional border clashes may occur, but protracted intense conflict is generally avoided unless an individual or group decides that the others can be controlled or eliminated. In addition, however, managers also look for opportunities to expand their territory by continual probing. But to prevent the loss of acquired territory, managers also develop defense systems.

When a new function is created, its birth is not a welcome event unless it is perceived as being necessary and beneficial and as not encroaching on others' territory. Operations managers may profess the need for a human resources function and publicly welcome its creation. However, privately, they may feel the opposite, because this newly created function will exercise influence or perhaps even control over their territory. If an existing human resources function has historically been viewed as an interloper or a necessary evil perpetrated on the organization by government or higher organizational authority, then expansion of its influence can hardly be welcomed by those who believe they are losing what they have worked hard for.

In an organization, the system of rewards and punishments significantly affects individual and group behavior. Leaders in organizations, whether the groups are formal or informal, influence the thinking of all organization members through the distribution of rewards and punishments. When executive-level management sanctions the activities of the human resources function, overt acceptance of it filters down the organization. To openly resist what has been sanctioned by the organization's primary leaders is political suicide and inadvisable unless one has a professional death wish or the actual power to resist. The safer course of action is to live with the decisions and when opportunities present themselves, limit their influence.

Reducing Conflict and Building Cooperation

Conflicts between human resources and other organizational groups are far less frequent when the function is created or its role expanded because operations, service, and other support groups perceive the need for it or its expansion and view it as truly beneficial. As long as human resources proves to be a net positive factor over and above the maintenance of power by these groups or individuals, it will be, at the least, accepted, and, at best, strongly supported.

As a staff, or support, function, human resources provides guidance to management. Whatever authority the human resources function has is derived from executive-level management. Human resources personnel are responsible for advising executive-level management as to the need for developing new, or revising current, employment and employee-relations policies, procedures, and practices. They are responsible for keeping management up to date on changes in the internal and external environments. To the degree that management gives it the expressed or implied authority, human resources has the responsibility for ensuring that all levels of management use their authority in a manner consistent with the organization's policies and procedures. However, when human resources has the authority to amend or rescind decisions made by managers below the executive level, conflict is unavoidable.

It must be remembered, however, that it is impossible to delineate all policies and procedures with such precision that no misinterpretation occurs. It is also impossible to cover all conceivable employment and employee-relations situations. In fact, even to attempt to do so would be impractical and bureaucratic.

Additionally, many decisions require the use of judgment, and judgment always has a large measure of subjectivity built into it, making written policies useless or even detrimental in some cases.

While conflict between management and the human resources function is unavoidable, it does not have to be destructive. It is important to remember that conflict can be channeled to ignite creativity. While human resources may not always share management's view, both share certain interests. Operations, service, and all support functions, including human resources, exist to serve the needs of the organization. The organization, in turn, exists to serve the needs of society, employees, and others. Thus, all organizational functions are concerned with people, primarily employees.

It is important to recognize that human resources is a staff function. Its purpose is not to replace managers, but to help them be more effective, to avoid situations with employees that could cause problems, and to help bail them out when, on those theoretically infrequent occasions, trouble occurs. Managers, however, tend to throw up barriers to resist cooperation instead of looking for ways to facilitate it. Human resources, like most other things when attacked, looks for ways to defend itself. The result is continual, destructive conflict.

Building the Foundation of Cooperation

In any working relationship, it is important that each party understand and accept the role, responsibilities, and expectations of the other. Misunderstandings that could have been avoided or resolved through negotiation are a primary source of continued, unnecessary, and destructive conflict. Managers, as professionals, must often suppress personal feelings for the sake of their working relationships with others. The essence of teamwork is cooperation, which can only be achieved when people learn to accept one another even though they may not particularly like one another.

Personality is a factor in the choice of a profession and even in the choice of an employer. Developing skills through training and experience influences the way people think, feel, act, and react. People tend to seek information and support that reinforces their beliefs and reject whatever threatens them. Beliefs, values, attitudes, and whatever else they may be called shape behavior. Production, marketing, finance, engineering, administration, quality control, legal, and human resources specialists all view the organization and each other's role in it from different perspectives. When perspectives differ, misunderstandings can result. Rather than work toward minimization or resolution of misunderstanding, which can be painful, people often choose avoidance as the path of convenience. Even worse, if avoidance is not practical or not maintainable, then divisiveness is the frequently chosen course of action. Figure 1 depicts the kind of organizational environment that exists when cooperation collapses.

How to Reduce Conflict

Managers should accept the fact that within the organization, all functions share some common concerns and yet have certain unique interests. Common interests should be identified and agreed on. Unique interests should also be identified and thoroughly discussed in a neutral environment, preferably away from the organization, with the objective of helping each function to understand the others. Accepting different roles and understanding how they interface with one another is the key to cooperation.

Managers should also accept the fact that the human resources function is not going to go away. If anything, its influence is likely to expand. The important thing is to make it work to support other functions in meeting their responsibilities. As long as managers use their authority in ways that are consistent with established employment and employee-relations policies, procedures, and practices, human resources personnel will have no legitimate reason to encroach on managers' territory. Human resources can only recommend policy. Executive-level management must approve it. Policies embody the philosophy of the organization's

Figure 1. Organizational conflict.

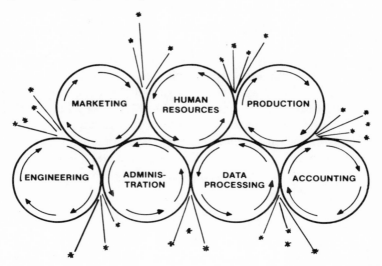

executive leadership. It is ignoring or misapplying policies, procedures, and practices by managers that openly invites human resources to expand its control. Executive-level management will sanction this action because of its need to have consistency and maintain control.

Managers need to exercise sound judgment in making decisions. If they allow their judgment to be clouded by emotions and personal biases or prejudices, human resources will be given the authority to develop, implement, and administer additional controls. In any organization where authority is somewhat decentralized, written policies and procedures are necessary in order to avoid serious inconsistencies in decision making and subsequent loss of control. Written policies outline the framework for decision making. However, this framework can be very broad, allowing for considerable flexibility, or it can be extremely narrow, allowing for virtually none.

Because of increased specialization in all fields, it is impossible for most people to have extensive training in more than a few areas of knowledge. Unfortunately, though, failure to understand what the other person is talking about invariably causes problems. People in staff functions such as human resources all too frequently have little understanding or appreciation of the other organizational functions over which they exercise influence. The same can be said of operations personnel. This condition can be changed, however. Through cross-training, career pathing, meetings, seminars, project teams, and by other means, people in key positions can learn enough about the other organizational functions they interact with to develop a proper understanding of how the organization functions as a whole.

Summary

The purpose of this chapter has been to help managers understand more about their own organizational role as trustees of responsibilities who must continually respond to changing conditions. Managing is a complex activity and a challenging profession. Given the fact that we live in a constantly changing world, managers need to capitalize on the skills of specialists from all types of disciplines to meet the opportunities and challenges of the 1980s and beyond. People are essential to nearly all organizations, and without a continuing high level of cooperation from all its members, an organization finds its goals more difficult, if not impossible, to reach. Human resources personnel have specialized training, which if put to proper use, can greatly facilitate management's efforts. It is time to utilize their skills to the fullest. Each of the remaining chapters in this book focuses on specific areas where managers can more effectively put to use the human resources function.

2

Using the Human Resources Function More Effectively to Attract, Select, Utilize, and Retain People

Most managers have had considerable experience in hiring people. It is a common process, one as old as the management process itself. Yet it has become increasingly difficult to attract good people. The problem is common to most organizations, but it can be resolved.

Why did this situation develop? How did it reach near crisis proportions? Considering the advanced state of modern management, why hasn't it been resolved before now? As important as the problem is, it is only one part of a larger set of problems that stem from failure to adequately orient the new employee to the organization, to the job, to the unit to which he or she has been assigned, and to what is generally expected of him or her. What should be an important concern has become largely form over substance, even though helping the employee to develop into a productive member of the organization is of vital importance to nearly every manager.

Clearly the attraction, selection, and utilization of people can be costly, ineffective, and frustrating to everyone involved. These problems are not insurmountable, however, and effective solutions are available. Some measures can be implemented at little expense to the organization and can, in fact, even result in cost savings. Managers, working in cooperation with human resources, hold the key. Human resources can provide the conceptual framework and support mechanisms to help the organization both avoid and resolve problems. Managers, to the extent they utilize these organizational supports, are ultimately responsible for their effective application. This chapter is designed to provide managers with a basis for evaluating their own strengths and weaknesses on these crucial issues as well as for defining approaches to increasing their effectiveness as managers.

Some Causes

Developing solutions that bring about lasting results requires understanding the causes of these problems. Some causes are of recent origin, while others are long-standing. Certain causes can be eliminated; others, at best have to be tolerated or accepted. They are as follows:

• Attitudes toward organizations, particularly large ones, have changed considerably. People's trust and confidence have eroded, and the public is increasingly wary of accepting and following without question an organization's established way of doing things.

• Conversely, some organizations continue to treat employees as just another dispensable resource to be used and discarded when their value has been consumed.

• Ironically, as people's expectations of what organizations should be doing for them have grown, their expectations of what they should be doing for organizations and others have decreased.

• Intervention by government through employment laws and

ations has substantially reduced management's flexibility in
ting and selecting people and in managing them.

When people are readily available, as in times of recession,
izations have fewer job openings. In prosperous times, jobs
n unfilled because of a lack of applicants.

or certain types of job skills such as electronic data process-
rganizations must compete aggressively for a limited num-
f applicants.

cting People to the Organization

overall effectiveness of the organization, but more
fically the effectiveness of its managers, begins with attracting the appropriate kinds of people. One can make an analogy
drawing on the manufacturing environment to illustrate this
point. A car fender is ultimately only as good as the metal chosen
to produce it. In other words, organizations spend enormous
sums of money to attract applicants, yet frequently find the results (the fender) less than desirable, because they have failed to
recruit employees of the quality they want. Attracting people is
often a costly, time-consuming, and frustrating activity.

The objective, then, is not just to attract people but to attract
those who are interested enough in the organization to seek employment and who possess the education, skills, and experience
that meet the requirements of available jobs. An increasingly important additional factor is the applicant's attitude and willingness to commit his or her talents to that organization.

Deciding on the kind of applicant needed begins with an activity not traditionally associated with the recruitment process—
employment planning. In its simplest form, employment planning
means determining the organization's present and projected
needs for people. Assessing the specific needs of a particular unit
in terms of number of people and desired education, skills, experience, and attitudes is up to the manager of the unit. Although

the human resources function can assist in employment planning, it is the manager who has the primary responsibility to know both the job needs and the job environment. Therefore, the effectiveness of human resources in supplying qualified applicants is directly related to the comprehensiveness of the employment-planning information supplied by managers.

After the employment-planning phase has been completed, it is up to human resources to design and implement recruitment activities and programs to successfully attract the desired applicants. An organization's ability to attract applicants is influenced by many factors, some of which are:

The organization's image or reputation as an attractive or unattractive place to work.
Competitiveness of its compensation package.
Opportunities for advancement.
Job security.
Funds available for recruitment.
Knowing where to look for applicants and how to attract their interest.

While human resources has the responsibility to seek out and attract qualified applicants, all too frequently managers are unaware of or are not concerned with this effort. Yet managers, of course, have a vested interest in its success. Some of the more typical recruitment activities engaged in by human resources are these:

RECRUITMENT PLANNING
Verifying with managers that the existing job descriptions and specifications accurately reflect the organizational unit's needs.
Reviewing the education, skills, experience, and other qualifications a likely applicant should possess; if compromises must be made because of scarcity of qualified people, determining in what areas and to what extent.

Determining likely sources of applicants.

Establishing a recruitment budget.

Preparing recruitment material, including literature, audio-visual assists, and other items.

Designing and writing ad copy for newspapers and trade journals.

Clarifying whether it is appropriate for the manager to accompany the recruiter on initial interviews.

IMPLEMENTATION

Contacting public and private recruitment agencies, professional associations, and colleges; use of current employees to assist in referring applicants should be considered.

Scheduling and conducting preliminary screening interviews.

Giving appropriate feedback to managers.

Agreeing on applicants to be referred to managers for interviews.

Two primary considerations that help shape recruitment activity are the level of the job opening and the number of qualified people available. The effectiveness of the hiring process depends considerably on the effectiveness of this attraction/recruitment process. Any initial impression is influenced by how the applicant perceives the organization. In fact, the potential employer-employee relationship begins with that first impression, which affects both its success and longevity. Studies show that applicants who form unfavorable initial impressions, even though they accept the job offer, frequently become dissatisfied employees, expressing their discontent in absenteeism and unrest, which usually result in many other undesirable problems including high turnover.

As simple and routine as some aspects of the recruitment process appear, all too frequently they fail to produce the desired results. Either human resources does not fulfill its responsibility, or management fails to determine what it wants, or both fail to cooperate with each other. A common mistake made by human resources, particularly in smaller organizations where a limited number of human resources personnel perform many diverse activities, is to hurriedly attempt to fill a job vacancy without properly planning a coordinated recruitment effort. This shotgun approach frequently consumes more of everyone's time and more of the organization's money—and produces less desirable results—than would have been achieved through proper planning. On the other hand, many managers rely too much on human resources. Managers should not hesitate to question human resources about the proposed recruitment plan and should feel free to disagree with its contents. In the selection process, managers should judiciously determine what kind of applicant they are seeking. Often managers mistakenly believe that this decision is not their responsibility. When either human resources or management leaves too much of what should be its shared task to the other party, less than successful results are likely to occur.

Who Makes the Final Selection?

In some organizations, human resources is assigned the responsibility not only to recruit and screen applicants, but to make the actual hiring decisions. This is detrimental to the organization, because after hiring, human resources will have little direct contact with the employee. The employer-employee relationship will be formed and maintained by the manager. If managers have no voice in the hiring process, it is unlikely that they will enthusiastically accept the employee into their organizational unit. The relationship begins under a serious handicap.

The other extreme—excluding human resources from the selection process—also poses serious problems to the organization. Allowing individual managers to make the hiring decision alone encourages inconsistent hiring practices and biased selection. It also increases the likelihood of violations of regulations concerning equal employment opportunity, affirmative action, or other labor or civil rights law. Cooperative participation is essential to ensure that the process will achieve satisfactory results.

Even with a smooth-running process, however, not every new person hired will remain with the organization. This is not so much a reflection on the hiring process or on the organization as on today's employees. Modern society is highly mobile. People are not reluctant to move to distant geographic areas. Also, their reliance on the organization for financial security has decreased, as increased government and social welfare legislation have removed many of the financial problems attendant to risking unemployment. In addition, opportunities for growth and career development may be insufficient in some organizations. On the positive side, a certain amount of turnover can be healthy, allowing for an infusion of new talent.

The Selection Process

The actual beginning of the selection process occurs during the attraction phrase. The requisites for applicants stipulated in the ads, the selection of recruitment sources, and the questions asked in the preliminary interviews are designed to screen out the decidedly unqualified people.

Central to the selection process is the interview. The interview has always been essential, but it has become more critical as the organization's use of reference checks, background investigations, pre-employment testing, and application information has become restricted because of legislation and changing social attitudes. In addition, applicants are becoming more skillful in the interview process. These factors enhance the value of the interview process. A skillfully planned interview can produce the appropriate job-related information needed to make an intelligent hiring decision. The key to effective interviewing is to understand its purpose. Simply stated, an interview should allow managers to gain a reasonably accurate impression of the applicant's

Figure 2. Basic elements of the selection process.

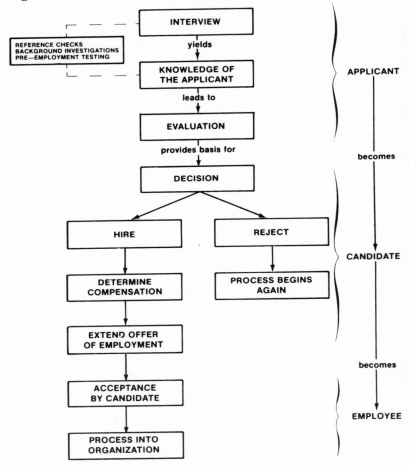

qualifications and abilities. This information forms the basis for some of the crucial selection-process decisions, incuding whether or not to extend an offer of employment, and if so, at what rate of compensation.

The various activities that constitute the selection process are illustrated in Figure 2.

Who does what and when in each step of the selection process is influenced by such factors as the organization's size, its traditions and past practices, and the scope of the responsibilities assigned to human resources. Naturally the level of the job, the constraints of time, and the competency and experience of the managers in interviewing and evaluating candidates play an important part, as well as the organization's current EEO goals and timetables.

Aside from these and other variables, selection is a shared responsibility of human resources and management. Human resources' responsibility for coordinating the entire effort, however, is clear cut.

The Interview

The interview activity begins by either bringing the applicant to the organization or sending a representative of the organization to the applicant. Except in such special circumstances as scarcity of applicants, most people applying for entry- or lower-level jobs are drawn from the local geographic market. Typically, they either apply in person or respond through some local intermediary, such as a newspaper advertisement or an employment service.

Higher-level jobs frequently require bringing applicants to the organization from distant geographic areas. If applicants are scarce, however, the organization may have to send representatives to the applicant's locale. Consistency of approach and wise use of the organization's money dictate that this phase of the interview activity be well coordinated. Human resources, by virtue of both its overall role and its involvement in the attraction process, is in the best position to provide this coordination.

Typically the activities to be coordinated are scheduling travel arrangements for the applicant's visit to the organization, arranging lodging accommodations, familiarizing the applicant with the local area, touring the organization's facilities, and processing the expenses incurred in conjunction with these activities as well as expenses incurred by the applicant that call for direct reimbursement. These and similar activities are best handled by human resources so that managers do not have to divert valuable time and effort from their regularly assigned duties. Aside from these considerations of cost and time, obviously the applicant must gain a favorable impression of the organization.

For applicants to entry- or other lower-level jobs, this is probably their first contact with the company. Even for applicants to higher-level jobs who have been exposed to the organization during recruitment, this second contact will either help to affirm a previously positive perception or serve as an opportunity to rectify a less than favorable impression. Even when an applicant is rejected, an organization should take care not to cause resentment. An organization's ability to attract future applicants, particularly in small communities, is sharply affected by the way it rejects present applicants.

Determining what information is needed and how to properly evaluate it to make a decision to hire or reject the applicant is the greatest source of difficulty to everyone. Interviews all too often fail to achieve their planned objectives and become little more than meaningless conversations. A thorough understanding of the education, skills, and experience needed by qualified applicants is essential to determine, first, what information is needed and then, what interview questions to ask. Two simple guidelines can help in formulating questions, namely, that they be strictly job related and that they be nondiscriminatory. The extent to which reference checks, background investigations, pre-employment tests, and other screening tools are then used depends on how much of the desired information has been gained in the interview.

Who will conduct the interview, what kind, and how many will be decided by the information needed. For entry- and other lower-level jobs, interviews can be reasonably standardized. It is usually easy to ascertain whether the applicant has the requisite qualifications for a clerk-typist or machine-operator position.

These interviews require little time. Most or all of the information needed to make a hiring decision can come from the initial interview, which should be conducted by human resources people. This is done not to exclude managers from the interview process but to relieve them of time-consuming initial screening activity. Successful applicants are then referred to the manager for further interviewing. An applicant should rarely be hired by human resources without involving the manager, either during this critical step or at any other step of the selection process.

In certain situations, notably higher-level jobs or jobs requiring special skills or knowledge that cannot be readily assessed during an interview, or in jobs requiring considerable team effort, an additional, effective interview tool is to have selected employees assist in the interview process. Their evaluation of the applicant can provide an additional and objective source of information. Employee involvement offers the added advantage of supporting managers in making a hiring decision. It also can facilitate the assimilation of the newly hired employee into the organization at a later point.

There should always be overlap between the interviews by human resources and managers. The degree of overlap usually depends on the job level. In positions on the clerk-typist or machine-operator level, human resources can obtain most of the desired information. The job specifications for these jobs involve mostly routine skills, such as typing, filing, or machine operation, and whether or not an applicant has them can be readily discerned. In higher-level jobs, where the tasks and duties are not so sharply defined and where such abstract skills and abilities as planning, directing, and controlling are required, it is more difficult to determine the extent to which the applicant has these qualifications. Moreover, the risk and cost involved in making a wrong hiring decision increases with the job level. Therefore at higher levels, the value of overlap between the interviews by human resources and managers is in sharing information and perceptions of the applicant's abilities and helping either affirm or change initial and subsequent impressions. In addition, the degree of overlap is also influenced by the fact that managers will usually interface more on a day-to-day basis with employees in higher-level jobs because of their shared activity and thus have a greater vested interest in knowing whom they are selecting. Again, human resources should plan how much overlap there should be and who will emphasize what key points in each interview.

Although the discussion thus far has concentrated on the organization's need for methods of gaining information from the applicant, a well-planned interview also allows for information to be given to the applicant to help him or her form a broader impression of the organization. By the same token, who gives what information to the applicant should be coordinated by human resources.

The kind of interview, that is, whether it is structured or informal, depends mostly on the job level. The structured approach of asking a standardized set of questions is most useful for lower-level or routine jobs. In higher-level jobs, the importance of skills in interpersonal relations and various abstract abilities increases, making it difficult to assess the applicant's technical expertise. Thus, interviews for higher-level jobs tend to be less structured, although there is a greater need to keep this kind of interview on track toward the planned objectives.

Whether interviews are conducted one-on-one or in a group setting or a combination is determined mainly by the job. Interviews for jobs involving extensive interfacing with other employees, customers, or outside groups are sometimes conducted in group settings where the applicant is subjected to group dynamics similar to what might be encountered on the job. Another advantage to group interviews is that several people can assess an applicant in one sitting. Group interviews require considerable planning and care in their execution to be successful. For one, they can be threatening to the applicant, particularly if handled improperly. Finally, gimmicks have no place in the interview process. Placing the applicant under undue stress, while popular in some organizations a few years ago, generally proved to be of no real value.

How effective managers are as interviewers, aside from the foregoing considerations, is influenced by what training and periodic follow-up guidance they receive. Human resources is the logical source for this training and guidance. In smaller organizations, where the human resources function may not include a formalized training and development activity, outside consultants are useful. In larger organizations, specialized personnel working in the human resources function are available. In either case, both assessing the need for interview training and approaches to providing it are the responsibilities of human resources. As employment laws and regulations change, it becomes their job to keep managers informed of these developments as they affect the interview and selection process.

Screening Devices

While the interview is the key factor in the selection process, reference checks, background investigations, and pre-employment testing are extra, traditional sources that aid in screening. With the enactment of privacy laws, however, many organizations are becoming very reluctant to release information about former employees. Even credit bureaus and similar organizations have difficulty in obtaining complete, accurate, and relevant information. Whatever information is released is usually so limited as to have no real value. This declining availability is not really as detrimental as it appears. In the past, much of the data gleaned was highly subjective and of questionable applicability to the job for which the applicant was being interviewed.

If an organization receives or wishes to obtain a reference check, human resources, because of its familiarity with the applicable laws, should be responsible for processing it, whether the request is for information on its own former employees or on an employee of some other organization. Requests for information about employees should always be referred to human resources.

Pre-employment testing has also diminished because of various laws and regulations. Even before these laws were enacted, the role of testing was misunderstood. Results were often the deciding factor in the selection process, relegating the interview to secondary importance. Testing presents problems—deciding what to measure, how to measure it, and how to weight it in the selection process. The higher the level of job, the more difficult it is to devise a test that is both job validated and is reliable. Test validation is complex, costly, and time consuming. In addition, higher-level jobs are qualitatively oriented, making it difficult to establish what should be included in an appropriate test or what the standards of measurement are. Skills such as typing or manual dexterity for operating a machine can be more easily measured by tests. Again, though, the question of what the standards of measurement are must be raised. It is our belief that while testing may have value, that value is in proportion to the results expected and the value attached to those results in the selection process.

Evaluation of Applicants

Evaluation serves as a bridge between obtaining information about the applicant and doing something with that information. It is a time to reflect on what has occurred thus far in the selection process before proceeding to make the all-important hiring decision. In order to arrive at an appropriate decision, all the information from the interviews and from reference checks, background investigation, pre-employment tests, and similar sources must be assembled and coordinated. This information should be placed in some kind of order for presentation to management, who will make the final hiring decision.

The coordination and summarization of information is appropriately the role of human resources. Assuming that it has coordinated the previous processes of recruiting, interviewing, and screening, the task is a logical extension of these activities, also leaving managers free for production-oriented activities. Managers should be familiar, however, with both what human resources does and how well it does it, particularly this critical step in the selection process. It is important that information about the applicant be as accurate as possible, complete, and relevant to the job opening.

Evaluation is critical to the selection process. The success of hiring decisions is in direct proportion to the accuracy, completeness, and relevancy of the information gathered on the applicants. If information is found to be incomplete or inaccurate, it will be quickly revealed in the evaluation process. In any event, selection should be held off until these issues are resolved. Decision makers need to rely on what is *known,* not what is unknown. Evaluation then, is an information-oriented process. It provides the framework within which to make the hiring decision. Hunches, intuition, or "gut" feelings about applicants may be correct, but they are not defensible in decision making. Also, they make the organization more vulnerable to charges of employment law violations. The evaluation process also serves as a check on how well the previous processes of attracting, interviewing, and screening have been carried out.

The Hiring Decision

The hiring decision is the moment of truth in the selection process. Hiring the wrong candidate can result in problems ranging from difficult to disastrous, and it can cost the organization untold sums of money, frustrate the manager, and—especially important—result in the loss of a better candidate. At best, it is a process that involves risks. The objective is to reduce the risks through use of good decision-making techniques. Here are some practical guidelines:

• Do not attempt to find the perfect candidate who possesses the education, skills, experience, and other qualifications that exactly fit the job specifications. Rarely, if ever, does that person exist.

• Particularly in higher-level jobs, recognize that each candidate possesses certain unique talents and abilities that influence both the composition of the job and its contribution to the organization. In some instances it may be better to modify jobs to fit people, as opposed to modifying people to fit jobs.

• The hiring process is one of compromise, particularly as it applies to higher-level jobs. Know where to compromise and how much.

All activity pertaining to the hiring decision is influenced by the answers to these questions: Does the candidate meet the job specifications and the organization's needs? Does the organization meet the candidate's needs and expectations? Can the organization meet the candidate's compensation and other requirements?

In evaluating candidates' education, skills, experience, and other related qualifications, consideration must be given not only to how well they meet the job requirements, but also to how well they fill the future growth needs of the organization. For certain jobs offering limited growth, the candidate's potential may not be an important issue. Just as certain jobs are limited in what they can provide, not everyone desires to grow with the organization. Other jobs in more technical areas or in rapid-growth environments demand that candidates possess additional potential beyond what is necessary to perform the present job. This question must be carefully assessed.

Because of many economic and social influences, not every candidate will accept an offer of employment. A candidate's initial interest in the organization does not guarantee acceptance of a job offer. Just as the organization evaluates candidates, so do candidates evaluate organizations. Particularly in times of low unemployment or in cases of jobs involving much-needed specialized skills such as data processing or certain types of engineering, candidates are often highly selective. Conversely, organizations, too, should be selective. For example, not all candidates have well-defined career goals. Frequently, the organization must assess what the candidate's present interests are and then project what their interests, needs, and goals for the future are likely to be. This is especially true if long-term relationships are desired.

Perhaps the most sensitive issue in the hiring decision is salary. Salary is frequently the major obstacle for both parties and is often why the candidate does not receive an offer, or why, if received, the offer is rejected. Establishing a salary offer requires that a delicate balance be maintained among offering what the candidate wants, what the market dictates the organization will have to pay, and how that salary will interface with the salaries of existing employees performing the same or similar kinds of work.

In establishing a salary offer, consideration must be given to its flexibility. Depending on the organization's policy on salary negotiations, limits should be established regarding the range of the offer. In lower-level jobs, especially when skilled candidates are readily available, there may be only a small range of negotiation, if any at all. In higher-level jobs or highly competitive market conditions, a greater range is usually necessary. Benefits and perquisites may also be negotiable in higher-level jobs, which tend to be more personalized and have more varied compensation packages.

Particularly in the hiring decision there should be shared involvement and close cooperation between human resources and managers. As a support function that serves not only managers but the total organization, human resources has the responsibility to monitor and guide the organization's hiring practices to ensure consistent compliance with equal employment opportunity requirements, organizational policy, and the letter and spirit of the law.

Extending the Offer of Employment
Extending the offer of employment philosophically involves considerably more than just offering a job with a certain salary and benefits. In one sense, offering a job is a mechanical function,

but by itself it is incomplete. Granted, the job, salary, and benefits are important. Beyond these, however, the focal point of offering employment is on the broader issue of offering a working relationship. The degree of interest an organization has in its employees determines to a great extent the success of this relationship. During the interview process, an applicant usually gets a glimpse of the value an organization places on its employees. Whether that initial perception is valid, the actual strength of the organization's interest will be more significantly evidenced to the candidate by the offer of employment process.

In extending the offer of employment, then, organizations should make a point to demonstrate this interest, through discussion of the organization's practices regarding education and training, career development, and generally those other activities designed to help employees realize their goals while increasing their value to the organization. By the same token, consideration should be given to the employee's potential to grow with the organization, depending on the job level. This point is supported by studies showing that a good job with competitive salary and benefits is sometimes not enough to maintain the enthusiastic commitment of employees. The job, salary, and benefits may be sufficient to attract candidates, but much more is required to elicit their enthusiasm and commitment. If employees feel that the organization places little value on them, problems ranging from employee unrest to high turnover are almost bound to occur.

Who makes the offer of employment is not nearly as important as how it is made. Generally, offers for lower-level jobs are made by human resources, while higher-level job offers are made by managers together with human resources. A simple phone call or face-to-face conversation is appropriate in lower-level jobs. In higher-level jobs where the offer may involve agreements beyond the standard compensation package, making the offer face to face, with a follow-up letter outlining the agreement, is advisable. In all instances, human resources should provide counsel and guidance.

Processing the New Employee

This phase of the selection process is intended to facilitate the assimilation of the employee into the organization, and, as required, into the community. While orientation is the mainstay of processing the new employee, other activities are necessary as influenced by the job level and geographic relocation.

If a geograhic relocation is involved, the company should provide assistance in selling the employee's home and obtaining a new one and, in the interim, making temporary living arrangements. The organization can help coordinate the physical move of household goods, assist in making home-loan arrangements, and provide advice on schools, day-care centers, attorneys, physicians, dentists, banks, and other community services. There are other helpful things that can be done such as providing information on driver's license, car registration and inspection regulations, and special motor vehicle laws; helping the employee's spouse find employment; and familiarizing employees and their families with the location of shopping areas and recreational and social facilities.

Orientation is the focal point of the processing activity. It is also the activity in the selection process that is most misunderstood and taken for granted. Organizations spend vast sums of money and commit considerable amounts of their people's time and effort to attracting, screening, and hiring candidates, yet pay little attention to them once they are on the job. No relationship can be taken for granted, particularly a business relationship that is highly dependent for its success on an understanding by each party of the respective responsibilities as well as the benefits of the partnership. In fact, the effective utilization of employees, which will be discussed later in this chapter, actually begins with processing and orientation. Employees' perceptions of the organization's regard for them is largely influenced by this process.

Orientation is a time for the employee to become better acquainted with the organization and the organization to get to know the employee better. It is a continuation of what was initiated during the attraction and interview process. Unlike that process, however, where the objective is to exchange information so both parties can make a qualified decision about the other, the exchange of information during the orientation process is aimed at cementing the newly formed relationship and making it productive, mutually beneficial, and lasting. Since the organization already has considerable information on the employee, there is little immediate need for additional data except that required to process payroll and other information that was unavailable earlier because of privacy laws. On the other hand, employees are at a disadvantage. They often know relatively little about the organization, its products or services, its philosophy of operation, and where they fit in. Before they can truly become productive, they need to be given certain information.

Regardless of how educated, experienced, or mature new employees are or the level of the job, the transition to a new environment, even under the best of conditions, is an anxiety-producing experience. Unfortunately there is little a new employee can do to reduce that anxiety. Clearly, the organization has to play the senior role in the developing relationship. Only it can provide the proper information, and only it can take the appropriate measures to reduce the anxiety in new employees and ensure that their transition into the organization is a positive experience.

Although the organization has these responsibilities, it has all too few initial opportunities in which to exercise them. First impressions that have been made during the orientation process are long lasting and they are frequently correct. They are, moreover, difficult to change. Many organizations experiencing high turnover can trace their difficulties to an ill-defined orientation process.

Orientation is anything but informal. It should not be taken for granted. Its success, as ultimately measured in productive employees, is in direct proportion to the amount of planning and care it receives. Specifically, in planning the orientation process, ask these questions:

- What general information does the employee need to function in the organization?
- What specific information does the employee need to perform a given job?
- Who will convey this information?
- Are the people who are assigned the responsibility for communicating the information trained for their task and are they effective?
- What are the sequence and the timing for giving the information?
- Are there mechanisms to measure how much information employees have received and whether they understand it?
- Are opportunities provided for employees to ask questions and to give feedback?
- Is the overall effectiveness of the orientation process evaluated periodically and revised accordingly?

The comprehensiveness and sophistication of the orientation process varies with the organization's size and philosophy. In larger organizations, which have the benefit of highly specialized staffs and larger budgets, orientation is typically a very formal and planned process. This is not to say that smaller organizations cannot develop equally effective orientation programs. The effectiveness lies not so much in how sophisticated the techniques for presenting the information are, but rather in how thorough and relevant the material is. Certain items of information are basic to any orientation program:

- Information about the organization, its background, its future, products manufactured or services rendered, operating philosophy, comparison to similar organizations.
- Information about the organizational unit to which the employee has been assigned, how it is vital to the rest of the organization, and procedures and rules specific to it.
- Information about the specific job, special operating procedures, safety rules, and similar considerations.

- General information such as selected personnel policies, pay practices, location of lunch rooms, rest rooms, infirmary facilities.

One of the most important considerations in the orientation process is who does what. Recognizing that the objective of orientation is to ensure acclimatization and assimilation of employees, both human resources and managers have a vested interest in its success. Managers, however, have the greater interest. The effectiveness of the employee and ultimately of the employer-employee relationship is in no small way influenced by the orientation process. While it is principally human resources' responsibility to plan, design, and monitor the orientation process, its implementation is clearly a shared responsibility. Usually, human resources deals with all the information and activity of a general nature, such as the processing of paperwork for payroll and personnel records, discussion of the organization's history, its products, and the like. The value of human resources involvement is twofold: That department is in the best position to convey certain information in a consistent manner, and it can save the manager's time in so doing.

Managers typically furnish employees with certain specialized information pertaining to the job and the work environment. Selected involvement of managers is crucial. The success of the employer-employee relationship hinges on the kind of communication developed by managers with their employees during the orientation process. Managers who have daily contact with their employees are in the best position to establish the high level of communication necessary for any relationship to be mutually beneficial. An important ingredient often overlooked is feedback to employees regarding their progress. Additionally, information received by human resources or managers regarding the employee's progress or lack thereof should be shared with each other. When this is done, the employee is better assured of receiving assistance if needed.

Depending again on the job level or the specialized nature of certain duties of the job, management may involve other employees in the orientation process. This involvement ranges from assigning an experienced employee to tour the facilities with the new employee to more sophisticated activities, such as explaining specific job functions. Involving other employees can be useful. It gives them a sense of involvement in the organizational unit, and it increases the likelihood of their more readily accepting the new employee into their ranks. The new employee also benefits by becoming quickly familiar with the employee group.

While some aspects of orientation, such as communications, never end (in fact, they grow), the orientation phase is usually designed to coincide with the probation period. In the absence of a specified probation period, the length of orientation is typically between 60 and 90 days, during which time the activity described here takes place.

Utilizing and Keeping People

Organizations spend large sums of money to attract and hire people. Needless to say, organizations cannot function without employees. Oddly enough, though, far too many organizations lead employees to conclude that they are of secondary importance. Rather than maximize the investment of both time and money made in selecting an employee, some organizations tend to ignore that investment. The resulting underutilization and misutilization of employees are two of the most serious problems plaguing organizations.

Underutilization and misutilization are not only costly, but they can threaten the organization's very existence. At best, the situation is frustrating to employees as well as to managers. Employee salaries, benefits, and related expenses consume an ever-increasing percentage of total revenue. Conversely, productivity has been declining for nearly a decade. Even a well-managed organization faces uncertainty and difficulty, and a poorly managed one is almost bound to encounter problems.

Why do these problems exist? Can they be resolved? How? Underutilization and related problems exist primarily because management by and large has failed to include employees as an integral and major part of the organization. As illustrations:

- Meaningful employee input is frequently not requested or is overlooked.
- Sometimes employees are, in fact, overtly or covertly penalized for their input.
- Salary systems, increases, promotions, and the like often fail to reward employees for their contribution as expressed through their job performance.
- Restrictive personnel policies frequently attempt to bend employees to fit the job.
- Restrictive union agreements reduce the flexibility of managers by legislating that promotion and salary increases be given on the basis of seniority rather than merit.
- Programs to handle employees' concerns, problems, or complaints are often ineffective or nonexistent.
- Timely and accurate feedback to employees is frequently lacking.
- Use of employee involvement to resolve production or other organizational problems rarely occurs.

In addition, most organizations strongly emphasize the value of production to their managers, with the result that managers become so focused on productivity that they overlook the process by which productivity is achieved. And managers are reinforced in this attitude, since their own salary increases, bonuses, and promotions are strongly influenced or solely determined by their unit's productivity. Sometimes, the emphasis on production is so great that employees are viewed more as machines than as individuals with needs, desires, goals, and problems. This criticism is offered not to question the value of productivity but to advocate that productivity be increased by focusing on the agents through which it is achieved.

While the problem of underutilization and misutilization is complex and serious, much can be done to reduce it with reasonably little effort. As a staff function, human resources can provide advice and other support mechanisms, but clearly these problems are best resolved by managers, who are the key to the employer-employee relationship, which ultimately influences utilization.

A starting point for managers in any assessment of employee utilization is to examine how aware they are of each employee as an individual. Are employees viewed primarily through their job role as file clerk or machine operator or as persons? Developing sensitivity to employees as individuals is conducive to increasing awareness by managers of the talents, needs, and aspirations of staff members and thus increasing the likelihood of those talents being better utilized in the organization.

Are employees rewarded for good job performance? Managers should reflect on how they grant salary increases. If the organization has a compensation program that rewards employees for job performance, is it practiced by managers? To reward employees for anything other than job performance quickly discourages commitment, increases counterproductive game playing, and frequently curbs initiative and encourages mediocrity.

As jobs change, are employees encouraged or given the opportunity to develop the necessary new skills and apply for newly created jobs? How supportive are managers of employees who do not have the ability to develop skills? Are there other places in the organization where these people can be effectively utilized?

How favorably do managers look on the promotion of their employees to other units within the organization? Discouraging promotional opportunity or otherwise attempting to inhibit employees' professional growth only causes frustration in employees and increases the likelihood of their leaving the organization or, if they stay, becoming apathetic or counterproductive.

Is feedback regarding job performance given to employees in a timely manner? Particularly in this area, managers must realize that just as they have needs for feedback and affirmation, so do their employees. Feedback costs little to give, but is very costly when not given. To be effective, feedback must be continually offered.

Are managers available to their employees? Or are employees' questions viewed as annoying interruptions? Managers are the major link between employees and the organization. When this link is weak, the employer-employee relationship suffers, forcing the employee to seek alternative courses of action.

Are employees encouraged to share their opinions with managers? If so, are these opinions acted on, as they relate to improving the job or job environment? Employees can be a tremendous source of assistance, and involving them in this way can increase their enthusiasm and commitment, while job performance improves.

Are employees cross-trained to do more than one job? If so, both the organization and the employee will benefit—employees increase their versatility and value to the organization and usually become more secure, confident, and committed to their jobs, and organizations gain in many ways by increasing the availability of certain skills.

It is as important to understand why employees stay as it is to understand why they leave. Concentrating on why employees leave is not necessarily going to help the remaining employees. The reasons for leaving are usually biased and, therefore, suspect, whereas reasons for staying on a job are usually positive. The information is more reliable and helpful in designing programs that reinforce the organization's strong points and ultimately benefit the employee.

Employees' productivity and commitment depend on how they perceive what is expected of them and how the organization rewards them. These perceptions are shaped by a variety of influences, internal and external to the organization. A primary internal influence is the nature of the employer-employee relationship as maintained by the employee's immediate supervisor. Good working relationships do not evolve as a natural process. They must be cultivated and maintained.

In the long term, however, managers play the primary role in developing this relationship, and through their example they set the tone for maintaining it. The importance of a good employer-employee relationship is underscored by studies indicating that employees fail to be productive, not because they lack the necessary education, skills, and experience, but because their desire to perform the job is lacking. Much of the manager's job is to shape an environment conducive to increasing the employee's desire to be productive.

Lastly, all people have the need to be competent, to be good at whatever they do. How strong the need is may vary, but a feeling of competency is essential to the health and well-being of the human organism. If employees are properly selected, oriented, and utilized, the likelihood of their prematurely leaving the organization, either voluntarily or involuntarily, is greatly reduced. For the most part, employees will want to continue employment because they are satisfied with the working relationship and realize that little, if anything, could be gained by changing employers. In maintaining employment, employees benefit through professional growth and satisfaction of other work-related needs; organizations benefit by having dedicated, experienced, and productive employees. In turn, individual managers benefit because it is easier to supervise dedicated and competent employees, and human resources benefits because it has fulfilled its responsibilities as a staff function.

3

How the Human Resources Function Can Help You Manage Within the Letter and Spirit of the Law

Perhaps no topic is quite as complex as how to comply with the plethora of laws and regulations governing organizations. No matter what the organization's size, the geographic scope of its operations, or the products manufactured or services rendered, there seems to be a law to cover every facet of its operation. As regulated as our world now is, indications are that regulations will continue to proliferate. While the enactment of laws is aimed at addressing certain perceived needs, new laws often serve to identify or create an awareness of additional needs requiring even more laws. The cycle seems endless. In addition, bureaucracies created to administer and enforce these laws have an inherent tendency for self-perpetuation and expansion of size and power.

The difficulties that organizations, and more specifically managers, face in coping with legislation is made vividly clear in examining the regulations dealing with the broad issues of employment and employee relations. It has been said that more employment and employee-relations laws have been enacted within the past 18 years than during the previous 50 years. Is it any wonder that today's managers feel threatened, frustrated, and bewildered by these regulations and their impact—usually restrictive—on their jobs?

What can managers do to cope with this situation? What help and support are available to them? Are the laws and regulations as restrictive as they appear? Can certain laws actually assist managers in their role? This chapter will explore these questions. It is our belief that while the topic should rightfully be one of concern to managers, it is not as onerous as it seems.

A Brief Look at the Origin of Laws

Laws began with civilization. At first they were tacit, unwritten agreements. As civilization evolved, laws became more formalized and complex. Today laws cover almost every conceivable human activity. In addition, vast bureaucracies have been created to enforce them. Government, which makes and enforces them on federal, state, and local levels, is in fact one of the nation's largest employers. The purported purpose of laws is to provide a formal framework in which a society can function for the common good of its members. To what extent laws fulfill their purpose is largely a matter of the appropriateness of their intent, how well that intent is expressed, how effectively they are interpreted and enforced, and ultimately how strongly they are supported by society.

Of all the social forces that contributed to the growth of employment legislation in the United States, without a doubt the organized labor movement was the most significant. From the days of the American Revolution until the Great Depression of the 1930s, employee grievances were largely left to the individual courts. Judges, for the most part, were unsympathetic to workers, and consequently companies enjoyed virtually unchallenged power and autonomy in dealing with their employees. Unfortunately, as is to be expected, abuses became pervasive. Partly to extract protection against abuses of power, to seek more equitable treatment in pay, as well as to gain improvement in working conditions, and partly out of a desire to strike back in self-defense, employees sought ways to obtain strength in dealing with their employers. The result was the growth of labor unions and resulting legislation.

The most important of the labor laws were the Railway Labor Act of 1926, which acknowledged the right of railroad employees to join a labor organization; the Norris-LaGuardia Act of 1932, which expanded the freedoms granted in the Railway Labor Act to become federal public policy governing all workers; and the Wagner Act of 1935, which forbade organizations to interfere with labor-organizing activity and to discriminate against employees who engaged in such activity. From that beginning came literally hundreds of laws concerning fair employment, detailed controls over the relations between labor and management, training and development of workers, compensation and benefits, and workers' safety, health, and social welfare.

While the laws have grown in number and expanded to cover a larger jurisdiction of activities, they have also become increasingly complex and ambiguous. Not only do even the most experienced lawyers have difficulty in assessing what is "legal," but inconsistent interpretations of the laws by the various state and federal regulatory agencies, and even by the U.S. Supreme Court, only serve to confuse the organizations that must abide by them. Is it any wonder, then, that the mere mention of the subject is enough to give managers nightmares.

Response from Organizations to Regulations and Restrictions

As might be expected, organizations did not welcome the intrusion on their power and reacted accordingly, sometimes with success and oftentimes without. But what is past is past, and now

employment laws and regulatory machinery are firmly en-
sconced. The task then becomes twofold: to live within the laws
that are tolerable and to attempt to change those that are not. In
searching for ways to do that, organizations relied principally on
managers, with outside help from trade organizations, attorneys,
and other sources. As the number of laws increased and became
more complex, managers found themselves less and less able to
deal with them. This situation was not so much a reflection on the
competency of outside help or on managers, but rather a growing
recognition of the need to have counsel and support more readily
available and from a source that knows the organization inti-
mately and understands the particular laws and regulations affecting its operation.

This need is one of the major reasons for the growth of the
human resources function, which became responsible for compliance with the various record-keeping requirements imposed by
federal, state, and local legislation. Human resources, then, became known principally for its record-keeping and other routine
activities of limited significance. It was not until more recently
that human resources' additional potential value began to be recognized. Perhaps one of the major influences in creating this
awareness was the Civil Rights Act of 1964, which dramatically
brought new considerations to bear on organizations. As a result
of just this one law, organizations were required to answer to
more people, both in government and special-interest groups, and
to face the threat of court action for noncompliance, keep more
detailed records, and submit more reports. Aside from adjusting
its personnel practices, organizations also had to make changes in
its attitudes on some very traditional and sensitive issues such as
the role of women, minorities, and the handicapped in the work
world.

While the Civil Rights Act was the major piece of legislation of
that decade, it spurred the passage of lesser but still significant
laws dealing with a wide variety of new freedoms and entitle-
ments for employees. It also tremendously increased the general

public's sensitivity to the expanded rights of employees and of people in general. The 1960s were difficult times for many organizations.

In searching for more effective and readily available sources of assistance, organizations looked to the human resources function with mixed emotions. As stated earlier, human resources had been underestimated and underutilized by many organizations, and its role varied greatly, depending on the dictates of the organization. Beyond its gate-keeping duties, human resources shared few roles with management that could adequately form the basis for providing the specialized help now needed. Also, all too frequently the human resources function was staffed by people of limited ability, education, and experience, who had often been placed in that function because organizations did not know what else to do with them. Thus, organizations were unaware of just exactly what internal assistance was needed, and human resources, because of its narrowly defined role, was unable to either identify what was needed or provide it. Additionally, organizations were concerned about problems that might possibly result from allowing human resources, through expansion of its role, to encroach upon the previously uncontested authority of managers. Accordingly, organizations were reluctant to utilize the human resources function in these areas, but on the other hand saw no feasible alternatives.

At the same time, recognizing the growing need for specialized education for people working in human resources, colleges and universities began developing curricula that dealt with administrating the new laws on equal employment opportunity, equal pay, and the like. More people began to choose human resources as a profession, bringing specialized education and training into organizations. The end result was that organizations were able to benefit from this newly developed internal source of expertise, and the role of human resources was expanded.

Before discussing human resources' specific role in helping organizations deal with the new regulations, it should be reemphasized that human resources is a support, or service, function. In all cases, the primary responsibility for managing the organization rests with managers, at all levels. To be effective in their role, managers need to have reasonably complete authority, and if they exercise that authority judiciously and in compliance with existing legislation, intervention from human resources is unnecessary. However, when managers fail in their execution of this important responsibility, human resources may have to intervene. But it should do so only temporarily and remedially. The strength of organizations lies in the knowledge, experience, and applied practice of its managers. All organizational staff functions, particularly human resources, should support management's efforts. Accordingly, human resources, as a support function, should provide counsel, training, and assistance to managers but steadfastly avoid performing the managerial function. In essence, the roles of managers and human resources should complement, not duplicate, each other.

For this reason, organizations must carefully define the human resources role, principally by clarifying organizational needs and expectations. Additionally, that role should be explained to managers and employees. Lastly, executive management must lend its support and approval, which is critical to the acceptance of human resources' role by lower-level managers and employees.

Helping Organizations Cope with Employment and Employee-Relations Laws

Within the foregoing framework, then, one of the principal duties of human resources is to process information pertaining to existing and proposed laws and formulate suitable action and response. Regardless of the size or level of expertise of the human resources staff, this role should be a priority that is not compromised through either inappropriate staff selection or focus on activities of lower priority. The expansiveness of this important role is illustrated in Figure 3.

Figure 3.   Human resources as an information processor and action formulator.

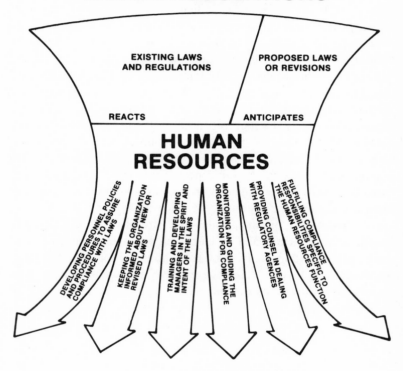

Before discussing each subfunction of this particular role, it should be emphasized that while one of the primary reasons for the evolution of human resources was to assist organizations in complying with the laws, additional purposes are served as well. For example, personnel policies and procedures also address the organization's need to maintain cooperative working relationships with its employees. The broader functions of this particular role should not be overlooked as we focus on its specific application to compliance with employment and employee-relations laws.

Developing Personnel Policies and Procedures to Ensure Compliance

Human resources serves as the organization's official, and often only, source of information pertaining to changes in existing labor laws and to requirements of new ones. Ignorance or failure to comply with these laws is not only indefensible but can cost organizations large amounts of money, time, and effort and can cripple its operation.

Since the requirements of these laws affect the operation of the organization, mechanisms—formal as well as unstructured—must exist to channel their influence in a way that is acceptable to the organization and also complies with the intent of the law. As an example, the equal employment opportunity laws required organizations in some instances to dramatically alter their hiring, pay, and promotion practices. A balance had to be reached whereby organizations complied with the letter and spirit of the law, while at the same time were able to incorporate the necessary changes into day-to-day practices without unduly upsetting the organization's operation.

This objective is accomplished by the formulation of policy. Just as operational policies are needed, so are policies that outline how organizations will deal with the many and varied issues pertaining to employment and employee relations. In smaller organizations, which tend to have informal structures, these policies may exist in practice only. In larger organizations, because of decentralized authority, multiple locations, difficulty in keeping managers up to date on current policy, and other factors, policies must be expressed in writing. Written policies provide some degree of assurance that the intent will not be misinterpreted and will be applied with reasonable consistency.

Policies, in essence, give broad direction throughout the organization and encourage management and employees to work toward that direction. Insofar as they pertain to the need for organizations to comply with regulations, policies establish how the organization will do so, who is responsible for ensuring that it will be done, and similar considerations. Typical policies would include such topics as equal employment opportunity, affirmative action, how overtime and other pay practices are handled, safety practices, and working conditions. It is up to human resources to be aware of existing and proposed laws and how they affect the organization. They are further responsible for formulating appropriate policies for recommendation to executive management.

Although human resources is responsible for enforcing certain of these policies, the vast majority of employment and employee-relations policies are the province of managers and therefore require management's understanding and support. Accordingly, managers should review and provide input on these policies before they are implemented. All too often human resources bypasses managers in the policy formulation and review stages and simply hands them the completed product. Not surprisingly, managers are less than enthusiastic in their support of something they had little influence in shaping.

As organizations change, so should their policies. Frequent review of policies is necessary if they are to remain effective in accomplishing their specific purposes—not only compliance with the law but giving direction to the organization that is consistent with its evolving philosophy. Also, it should be recognized that some policies are designed for short-term objectives. Once their purpose has been fulfilled, they should be eliminated. It is human resources' responsibility to make certain that the policies are accurate, current, and pertinent.

While our discussion has focused on policy, a few comments about procedure will help clarify certain distinctions and explain how each is needed to increase the effectiveness of the other. Policy outlines what is to be done and some of the reasons why.

Procedure outlines how the policy objective is to be achieved and who is responsible. It provides the mechanics of how to accomplish or fulfill the policy. Although frequently confused by many managers, policy and procedure are two distinct but equally essential parts of any policy statement. Just as in the writing of policy, clarity and specificity are essential in the construction of procedures. Ambiguity weakens policies and procedures and can create more problems than the policies and procedures themselves were designed to resolve. To ensure the satisfactory functioning of the organization, particularly at the lower managerial levels, procedure should encourage decision making and action at the lowest possible managerial level.

Procedure, perhaps more than policy, limits managerial freedoms. In this area, human resources should not stress unduly its monitoring of managers' actions. As discussed earlier, a delicate balance of power must exist between line managers and human resources. This balance is defined generally by their roles but more specifically by day-to-day practices and attitudes that are largely shaped by procedures.

Keeping the Organization Informed about
New or Revised Laws

In its role as provider to the organization of outside information pertaining to revised and new federal, state, and local employment and employee-relations laws, and as formulator of action within the organization to assure compliance, human resources has responsibility for formulating personnel policies. But in some respects, formulation of policy to ensure compliance is only a small, but significant, part of human resources' total responsibility. Policy, by itself, does not ensure that managers will understand and support that policy or ultimately that the organization will be in compliance with the law. Lack of effective communication, often due to the organization's size, may typically be a festering problem. Because inadequate flow of information affects the organization's adherence to personnel policies, human resources must be sensitive to the problem and knowledgeable in methods to increase communication. On this issue, human resources should lead and educate the organization through its example.

Before discussing specific methods of informing managers, and sometimes employees as well, about regulations, it should be emphasized that knowing the reasons for these laws is just as important as familiarity with their content. All too frequently, human resources, perhaps because of expediency or lack of thorough understanding of a law's intent, will portray the restrictions as being greater than they are. Consequently, a negative view is almost bound to be formed by the managers, which affects their attitude and ultimately how willingly they carry out the laws.

Frequently it is not the law that is restrictive or harsh, but how it is enforced. This applies not only to managers' perceptions but also to those of the government agencies charged with enforcement. Actually, some laws have proved to be helpful to organizations. For example, until the late 1960s, some organizations had separate employment applications for males and females. Female applications typically asked for information about the applicant's skill and experience in typing, shorthand, and other clerical abilities, whereas male applications concentrated on more technical, administrative, and managerial qualifications. Not so long ago newspaper employment ads were classified as male and female. Consequently women, who constitute an increasingly large segment of the work force, were underutilized through restrictive employment-screening processes. This practice worked to the disadvantage of both women and the organizations that denied themselves access to a largely unused resource of talent, creativity, and career potential.

Human resources, then, has the obligation not only to inform the organization about the laws but also to educate it as to why they exist. It is principally through this kind of understanding that cooperative attitudes are developed. Whenever possible, a law's benefits to the organization and particularly its managers should be explained. In this respect, human resources serves as the internal interpreter of legislation. It must inform the organization of the basis for every law. To give managers the actual text of the law or other raw, uninterpreted data potentially causes more harm than good by creating confusion rather than imparting knowledge.

Small organizations that have a limited human resources staff often find it difficult to readily obtain current information about the laws. Consequently they are frequently bewildered about approaches to the subject and are confused or not fully informed, which may mean that they risk noncompliance and its consequences. Availability of information regarding employment and employee-relations laws is not the problem however; rather selectivity is.

With proper guidance, information can be found readily and at little cost. Most organizations belong to trade or other professional groups, many of which provide, as part of their membership services, information about the laws and their specific impact on member organizations. Usually included as well is information about proposed laws, whether their impact will be beneficial or not, and advice to member organizations about the input they should give to their legislators in either supporting, opposing, or modifying proposed laws. In addition, some trade organizations offer reference services ranging from giving tips on additional sources of information to providing limited counsel through their legal staff.

Also, a number of subscription services are available through private publishing firms as well as through the federal and state governments. The fee is usually higher for subscription services from private publishing firms, but the material often includes an interpretation of the law in addition to its actual text. Understandably, government sources frequently cannot provide this kind of in-depth information or provide an objective interpretation because of their role as enforcer of the laws. They should not, however, be excluded from the human resources' priority reading list. Whether government or private, both sources make data available on a timely basis, often as frequently as weekly. Besides trade organizations, subscription services are the best and most economical source of accurate and timely information.

Use of the organization's outside legal counsel should not be excluded. It should be used judiciously, mainly because of the cost. The principal benefit of legal counsel to the organization is the assistance and direction given on laws requiring special research and interpretation.

Trade magazines and a wide variety of human-resources-oriented journals also provide interpretations and general information. The main disadvantage of this source is lack of timeliness.

Lastly, using other organizations within the same industry or business as a source should not be overlooked. This alternative is particularly useful for smaller human resources staffs. While the applicability and accuracy of the information should not be equated with that provided by legal counsel, it can still give limited direction.

What human resources does with the information is perhaps more important than how it acquires it. Aside from its use in establishing personnel policies, much of the data is crucial to the effective and efficient day-to-day operation of the organization, at least insofar as the organization is required to ensure compliance with the law. Beyond its effect on policies and procedures, information also shapes the organization's practices. Consequently, managers need to be kept advised and up to date.

The role of human resources in providing the relevant data in a timely manner is critical. To fulfill its responsibility, human resources can use a variety of formal and informal tools. The formal tools include special bulletins to managers outlining the highlights of a new law or revisions of existing laws, how they affect the organization, what the managers' responsibilities are in enforcing or complying with them, or what human resources' role is. Bulletins and similar written communiqués offer the advantage of quick distribution and also can be kept as reference documents. Their principal disadvantage is that they do not readily allow for additional clarification of the material or, of course, direct responses to questions.

Depending on the issues, meetings may serve as a supplement to previously distributed written communiqués or may be useful when it is felt that a more expansive form of communication is needed, as in the case of sensitive organizational issues created in part by the laws. Meetings are not always the most effective form of communication, however. They are time consuming and difficult to arrange so that all managers have an opportunity to attend, and frequently the information is lost in the emotional atmosphere developed by the discussion of sensitive issues.

Informally, human resources has many opportunities to provide information and, equally important, to help develop understanding about the intent and spirit of the laws through routine dealings with managers or on specific personnel issues for which managers are seeking assistance. Whatever mechanism is used, managers must be able to rely on it. Human resources has the responsibility to continually demonstrate its reliability by readily providing accurate, timely information.

Beyond keeping managers informed about the laws and their significance to the organization, human resources has the additional responsibility of informing employees. Whenever possible, we recommend that employees be advised by their managers of information pertaining not only to the laws but to other organizational issues. The more employees look upon their managers as the source of information, the stronger the manager-employee work relationship is likely to be. In certain instances, however, human resources can convey information more readily and economically. For example, employee handbooks and bulletin boards serve as two principal information sources for employees about employment and employee-relations laws that affect their organization's operation. Human resources is typically assigned the responsibility for the maintenance of these two sources.

Training and Developing Managers in the Spirit and Intent of the Laws

An additional, more structured, means of communication with managers on the subject of regulatory legislation is through training and development. In the process of informing managers, creating understanding, and fostering support, training and development pick up where the other previously discussed methods leave off. A degree of overlap in what each of the two subroles is intended to accomplish does exist, but there are also distinct differences. This is not to imply that training and development of managers is required each time a new law is enacted or existing ones are revised. As will be discussed in Chapter 5, training and development should be considered only in response to highly specific needs.

As it applies to ensuring compliance with the law, the principal aim of training and development is to alter managers' behavior through knowledge and understanding. In this respect, the use of information-dissemination methods discussed previously is limited. Clearly, the mere distribution of information is insufficient to change or otherwise influence managers' practices, many of which have evolved over a long period of time and are deeply ingrained. Also, training and development extend far beyond discussion of the spirit and intent of the law and its general impact on the organization. They focus on the specifics of new policies, procedures, and practices required for compliance.

Regardless of the organization's size and, more specifically, the number of staff members and the level of expertise in the human resources function, training and development should never be overlooked as an important communicator and shaper of the organization's attitudes and personnel practices.

Monitoring and Guiding the Organization for Compliance

Of the six subfunctions human resources performs in carrying out its responsibility as information processor and action formulator, without a doubt monitoring and guiding the organization for compliance is the most controversial and difficult one for managers to accept.

Differences between monitoring and guiding. At first glance, perhaps little difference can be seen between monitoring and guiding; there can be differences, however, both philosophically and in the manner in which each function is carried out. It is not a matter of choosing one over the other. Both are necessary.

Informally, human resources fulfills its monitoring function through its day-to-day contact with managers. In these routine relationships, the accent is not so much on monitoring as on providing guidance to managers on employment and employee-relations issues. The similarity between monitoring and guiding is that they have as their common objective compliance by managers with the organization's personnel policies. The difference is that monitoring is passive and is reactive oriented. It requires little skill. The authority given to human resources to carry out this role does most of the work.

Monitoring by itself is incomplete, and by itself cannot ensure compliance. It is relatively easy to hold managers accountable, but quite another matter to help them remain in compliance. Giving assistance, then, is the specific objective of guiding. As such, it is proactive and requires considerable skill on the part of the human resources staff and acceptance of their role by managers.

How monitoring is carried out. The major monitoring mechanisms are the organization's policies and procedures, both operational policies and those of human resources. As discussed earlier, both policies and procedures provide direction to the organization and limit freedom in making decisions. Equally important, they hold managers accountable for their decisions and actions. As the accountability process applies to personnel policies and procedures, managers become accountable for a wide variety of decisions and actions ranging from hiring, promotion, demotion, employment termination, and compensation. While ultimately they are accountable to the organization through its higher-level managers, the human resources function is charged with monitoring the total organization, particularly its managers, for compliance. Depending on the scope of the human resources function and how restrictive the policies and procedures are, both the monitoring role of human resources and that of enforcing the accountability of managers can be considerable.

In a broad sense, monitoring takes place at all levels throughout organizations. It is a basic responsibility of managers to monitor the performance of their employees as well as the functioning of the overall organizational unit. Monitoring is necessary to ensure that the direction of the organization is being followed, that productivity is being maintained, and generally that the organizational unit is functioning well. Beyond this level, the performance of a specific unit as well as that of its manager is monitored by higher-level management. Monitoring production levels and costs are examples.

While the monitoring of a manager's personnel practices by human resources is just one more form of monitoring, it has distinct differences. The principal one is that the managers who represent the organization's line functions are placed in the position of answering to staff. Also, human resources is frequently placed lower in the organizational structure, which means that higher-level managers are accountable on certain issues to a lower-level staff function.

Dealing with resentment. Throughout this book, we have maintained that human resources' overall role is one of staff support. In the realities of organizational life, however, few roles are that clearly defined. The very nature of the human resources function causes it to encroach upon managers' authority at different times and to differing degrees. Sometimes the formulation of personnel policies limits a manager's authority and freedom, but this form of encroachment is generally accepted by managers who realize the need to support the organization's policies.

There are, however, more direct forms of encroachment. Monitoring the practices of managers with regard to compliance with laws and the organization's own human resources policies is one example. The monitoring and guiding role causes perhaps the most concern to managers, partly for justifiable reasons. Although the role in itself is necessary and beneficial to the organization as a whole, difficulties frequently arise because of the way human resources carries out that role. Beyond these difficulties, however, the very fact of intervention creates resentment among managers that is difficult for human resources to overcome.

Typically, American managers are not inclined to ask for help, particularly from a staff function such as human resources and one that is frequently beneath their level in the organization hierarchy. Clearly, the burden is on human resources to prove its value as a guide to the organization. While a certain degree of monitoring is usually accepted—or, at the very least, grudgingly tolerated—by managers, guiding often is not. Through the reliability and type of assistance given, as well as how it is given, human resources must demonstrate its net worth as a source of guidance.

Importance of monitoring. These difficulties, however, do not diminish the importance of monitoring by human resources, both to assure compliance with the law and the organization's personnel policies and to see that uniformity is maintained in dealing with employees and related matters. In essence, monitoring also provides a check on the employer-employee relationship. Few, if any, feasible alternatives are available that would be as effective in protecting the organization from the risk of legal action resulting from noncompliance. Also, it is far better for the organization to monitor itself than to be monitored by the courts or regulatory agencies. Such possibilities are no longer remote. Several important court cases involving the failure of organizations to comply with affirmative action laws have resulted in the court's appointing itself as not only the monitor but the final decision maker regarding whom the organization can hire, promote, and terminate and what to pay employees.

Ideally, human resources should seek to develop a climate in which managers will think of it as a source of assistance and not be reluctant to ask for help. To accomplish this, the negative connotations of monitoring, such as the threat of reprisal and the tendency to judge managers as opposed to assessing the issues, must be overcome.

Providing Counsel in Dealing with Regulatory Agencies

While the preceding four subfunctions are intended to ensure compliance, even the most effectively run organization operates under the daily risk that an employee or some other allegedly aggrieved party will file charges against it with any one of the regulatory agencies. People are more prone now than in the past to take action seeking redress from organizations, even though there may be little basis for their action. Government regulatory agencies have made it very easy for people to file complaints and other charges. In addition, special-interest groups are available in some circumstances to provide assistance to the aggrieved party, ranging from advice to legal counsel and, in some instances, financial support for their cause. Lastly, while under our legal system the accused is innocent until proved guilty, frequently regulatory agencies are so imbued with the cause of the employee or other party filing the charges that they proceed as if the organization were guilty. As evidenced by verdicts and settlements, the U.S. courts and juries are frequently less than sympathetic with the organization's cause. Also, the reputation and credibility of organizations have suffered because of the hostile social climate toward business and institutions in general that prevailed during the late 1960s and early 1970s.

In addition to investigating charges, regulatory agencies may decide to audit the organization's employment and employee-relations practices. It is not uncommon for an organization to be investigated either in succession or simultaneously by the agencies charged with the enforcement of equal employment opportunity, affirmative action, OSHA, and the like.

The justification for such investigations is clear in light of the knowledge that much of the social legislation of the last 18 years was designed to protect workers and to give them expanded freedoms and rights and provide for redress when those freedoms and rights were denied. In any balance of power, when rights are given to one party the other party's freedoms are reduced. Accordingly, organizations have found themselves facing an ever-increasing number of restrictions. However, not all restrictions are harmful, and some are necessary to the common good of both organizations and society.

The restrictions and the laws supporting them must be obeyed as long as they are in effect. Abiding by labor and employee legislation is not always easy. As we have said, many laws exist, and many are extremely complex, so much so that even the regulatory agencies have difficulty in interpreting them consistently. By the very nature of many of the employment and employee-relations laws, organizations are placed in a defensive position and are therefore vulnerable. Under such circumstances, the only feasible alternative is to be prepared.

Unfortunately, too few organizations are as prepared as they could be. Consequently, both charges brought against them and audits by regulatory agencies are handled reactively. The risks involved are that the case preparation and the defense are handled improperly, that the action is disruptive to the organization's day-to-day operation, and that the chances of defending the charge or confining the audit are greatly diminished.

The human resources function is a readily available source of assistance. Aside from its role in developing and implementing preventive measures, human resources is responsibile for helping the organization deal with charges, audits, and other regulatory action. In their haste to seek outside counsel, organizations often fail to fully utilize this source. This is understandable since it was not until recent times that many human resources functions had the necessary expertise. Regardless of the size of the human resources staff, however, providing counsel and assistance in this area is a primary responsibility.

Human resources should be involved at the first sign of action by a regulatory agency. Its initial role is to identify the scope of the action and the issues involved, to assess the organization's liability and vulnerability, and to formulate an initial plan of action. From the beginning, human resources should be the organization's coordinator. In essence, all matters pertaining to the processing of charges or related issues, contact with regulatory agencies or other parties, and release of information should be either handled directly by or coordinated by human resources.

Human resources should advise executive management as to what additional help is needed and when. A resource that should be immediately involved is legal counsel. All to often, organizations shield charges and issues from legal counsel until important options available initially are lost by delay. This attempt to cover up severely restricts legal counsel in effectively dealing with the matter.

Human resources should also keep the particular managers involved in the action fully informed throughout the proceedings. Additionally, it should provide support for those managers. This is not to imply that human resources or the organization should condone the actions of the managers that led to the charges if the charges have any validity; rather, it should work with the managers to preserve their specific value while the charges are being dealt with and their continued overall value as members of the organization's management team is being appraised. Managing under favorable conditions is at best not easy. In times of difficulty, as in combatting charges, it can become frustrating and lonely. Once the damage has been done, there is little to be gained by damning those involved.

After assessing the situation and formulating an initial plan of action, case preparation should begin. One of the objectives of case preparation is to gather detailed information to more precisely identify the organization's strengths and weaknesses in the particular issue. Together with executive management, the affected manager and legal counsel can then arrive at a preliminary decision whether to defend the charges or seek settlement. It goes without saying that these experiences have tremendous learning potential. They can provide an additional dimension in reshaping the organization's policies, procedures, and practices, in training its managers, and in implementing other measures to strengthen its effectiveness and efficiency.

Considerable attention and effort should be given to case preparation. All too often, an organization's position is either understated or mistated because of insufficient preparation. Consequently, the merits of the case are not fully grasped by the courts or other regulatory bodies assigned to review and pass judgment, thus increasing the possibility of a decision that is unfavorable. As an extension of its role as coordinator, human resources should oversee the preparation of the case through all phases ranging from data gathering to presentation.

In determining whether to negotiate an early settlement or defend the charges, human resources should assess the impact of either decision on the total organization. While organizations have a tendency to want to settle charges brought against it quickly for reasons of cost, convenience, and expediency, frequently such settlements create broader problems than those they attempt to resolve, because their impact on the total organization has not been fully considered.

In dealing with regulatory agencies on other issues, such as audits of the organization's hiring or promotion practices, managers should be able to rely on human resources to provide guidance and assume control. Human resources, by virtue of its role and staff expertise, should be the internal expert on the laws, their impact upon the organization, and where to go for additional help. Accordingly, it should be able to deal with regulatory agencies so that the agencies' informational requirements are met while the interests of the organization are protected.

Managers should never attempt to deal directly with regulatory agencies without the guidance of human resources. Because it cannot be assumed that the regulatory agencies will confine their audit or investigation to the subject of the initial inquiry, caution is required. Many examples could be cited where regulatory agencies, either left unrestrained or handled improperly, have subjected organizations to investigations that extended far beyond the limits of the initial inquiry. Aside from the internal time, effort, and costs involved in handling such an investigation, the risks are tremendously increased that the final outcome could subject the organization to costly settlements in terms of both the dollar value of the actual settlement and its impact on the organization's operations.

Fulfilling Compliance Responsibilities Specific to the Human Resources Function

The human resources function has a specific set of responsibilities that only it can fulfill. Much of this work is of the organizational-maintenance variety centering on filing reports and supplying other information required by the various laws. An example is the EEO-1 form which must be submitted annually, listing the number of employees in various job classifications as compared to the employees' sex, race, and other factors. The proper and timely performance of these tasks serves to ensure that the organization complies with the various government record-keeping requirements. While managers are typically not involved in these processes, they should be assured that the responsibilities are being met.

Prevention is less difficult and less costly than dealing with consequences of failure to comply. Human resources can help managers comply with the letter of the laws, but it is entirely up to managers to comply with their spirit and intent. Regardless of how much staff support is available, if managers do not grasp the significance of legislation and give active support and compliance, that staff support is of little use and ultimately the organization becomes vulnerable.

4

Getting the Most
from Your Organization's
Compensation-Management Program

Perhaps the most important and sensitive aspect of employee relations is what is commonly referred to as "wage and salary administration," or "compensation management." Compensation management, although it is the term least frequently used in practice, is the most appropriate one to identify that field of activities. For this reason, the term compensation management will be used throughout this chapter.

People look for, accept, and maintain employment with organizations for many reasons. One of the most important is the need for money. To argue that in our society money is not a major incentive for working is to deny reality. In American society, money is important because it has social and psychological, as well as economic, value. Its versatility allows its use as a medium of exchange for products and services that can satisfy a wide variety of needs. This is not to say that money is the only factor influencing job-related behavior. Many capable people have comprehensively researched such questions as why people work and what affects their behavior on the job. While the results of these studies have varied widely, factors other than money do exist. Our position is that money is one of the most powerful and effective influences of behavior at every organizational level.

All managers, whether in operations or service, must be sensitive to the feelings and needs of employees. All kinds of difficult-to-resolve problems arise when employees perceive that the organization's compensation program is either badly designed or unfairly administered. Unfortunately, many organizations go to great lengths to keep employees, including most managers, uninformed about compensation policies, procedures, and practices. When people do not understand something that concerns them, they either accept it on faith or become suspicious. When it comes to money, people are more likely to be suspicious than trusting, and when suspicions seem to be confirmed, problems surface.

In recent years, compensation management has been receiving considerable attention and, as a result, has had a broader influence on managerial decisions. In all likelihood, this trend will continue for at least the next few years. A number of factors account for this new emphasis:

High inflation eroding the purchasing power of take-home pay.
Rising expectations of people in regard to what they need or are entitled to.
Changes in tax laws and regulations.
Changing attitudes of employees about management's ability to manage a compensation program fairly.
Title VII of the Civil Rights Act of 1964 and the Equal Pay Act of 1963. Both recognize sex-based discrimination claims of unequal pay for equal work.
Intense competition in some industries and geographic regions of the country for certain types of job skills that are in limited supply.

Because money is so important to employees, managers must be concerned about all aspects of the compensation process, not just the giving of periodic raises. Where management lacks knowledge, is indifferent, or lacks a degree of control over compensation practices, its ability to effectively manage people is impaired.

Because most managers have a limited understanding of the scope and depth of activities within the purview of compensation management and frequently do not know how to effectively apply what they do understand, it seems worthwhile to define the key compensation-management activities as part of the discussion on how to obtain the maximum benefit from their use.

Before doing so, attention should be drawn to another major obstacle to managers' understanding of compensation management—the fact that compensation-management terminology lacks standardized definitions. For example, to some compensation people "job evaluation" is the overall process of determining the relative value of jobs and includes market pricing along with internal job-content analysis. To others, "job evaluation" is limited solely to internal ranking or job-content analysis.

In very broad terms, a properly designed compensation-management program has three main elements, job-content evaluation, salary structuring including benefits, and performance assessment. No compensation program is complete or can be effectively utilized without all three elements. However, before beginning the development of an effective compensation program, particularly evaluation of job content, job analysis must be undertaken. Essentially, job analysis is the collecting, analyzing, and recording of job-content data so that accurate descriptions of jobs can be written. Accurate, current, and complete job descriptions provide the cornerstone for all other compensation-management-related activities.

Job Analysis and Job Descriptions

All jobs in an organization must be accorded value relative to one another. The idea of a file clerk or a laborer having a higher

relative dollar value than a president would be illogical. Det[...]
and timely job descriptions outlining job duties and other f[...]
tions and, more important, the contribution the job should m[...]
to the organization, written in a standardized format, are ne[...]
sary for determining the relative value. A common shortcom[...]
of most job-evaluation systems is the absence of complete, [...]
rent, and accurate information about job content. This [...]
should be readily available in the form of a properly written j[...]
description for every job, with a summary of the job's general
characteristics, an outline of the primary responsibilities and
duties related to major functional areas, and an outline of the
desired or essential skills, experience, training, traits, and characteristics that job holders should possess. Sometimes the
identified, desired, or essential skills are described in a separate
document known as the job specification. Information needed for
writing job descriptions can be obtained by any one or a combination of the following methods: interviews, questionnaires, logs,
written narratives, diaries, or work plans, or by direct observation.

The responsibility for job analysis should be shared among
management, employees, and human resources personnel. Human resources should be responsible for designing the data col-
lection and analysis. The amount of employee participation
should be up to management. Because of the importance of job
descriptions to all other compensation-related activities, managers must exercise judgment and discretionary authority to ensure that job-content information is accurate before the job descriptions are finalized.

Job descriptions are useful to management for purposes other
than job evaluation, for example, in the attraction, selection, orientation, evaluation, training, and effective utilization of employees. They can also be used to explain management decisions
to outsiders—arbitrators, courts, government administrative
boards and agencies. Properly developed job descriptions are essential to defending an organization's human resources policies,
programs, and practices.

Understanding job content is necessary to knowing what kind of people to attract and select. The job description is also a tool for communicating job content to employees. In addition, with clear job descriptions it is much easier to develop performance standards or goals. Job descriptions are also important in planning utilization of human resources and in identifying training needs. Unfortunately, many managers, because they do not understand the full benefits of having good job descriptions, tend to view them with indifference or as another one of human resources' bureaucratic impositions upon their time.

Once job content is identified for all positions, then the jobs can be evaluated to determine their relative hierarchical value to the organization. Compensation of employees should be based on two major considerations: the value of the job itself irrespective of the job holder and the performance of the job holder, determined by comparison with some absolute or relative job-performance standards.

The Job-Content Evaluation Process

Job-content evaluation is the process of systematically determining the relative value of each job in the organization. Internal job evaluation pertains to the ranking of each job in the organization from highest to lowest. External job evaluation pertains to the monetary value assigned to each job as determined by the value placed on it by the market. Both internal and external job evaluation, contrary to what many consultants would have managers believe, is still far more an art than a science.

Many different types of job-evaluation systems are used, but none are precise in their ability to measure relative job-content values. This difficulty holds true especially when measuring higher-level jobs, where the incumbent's personality and unique skills often determine job content. Even though all job-evaluation methods—especially internal methods as we have defined the term—are imprecise, systematic job evaluation is an activity essential to the development of an effective compensation-management program.

The Internal Job-Evaluation Process

Internal job-evaluation programs, whatever their specific names, fall into one of two categories: nonquantitative, whole-job evaluation and quantitative factor evaluation. The whole-job approaches, which are generally either simple ranking or slotting of jobs into prescribed salary levels, ranges, or grades, are easier to use than the factor-evaluation methods and can produce the same quality of results if management knows all job contents well. However, when jobs change significantly, especially because of the impact of technology, and management is unfamiliar with their content, the whole-job methods usually do not work very well.

The factor methods have the advantage that when properly used they require more rigorous analysis and as a result can provide more complete and more accurate information. These quantitative methods emphasize separating the job into each of the factors on which the organization places value and for which it is willing to pay, and then individually evaluating each of those factors. Typical compensable factors are skill, effort, responsibility, and working conditions, or minor variations of these. At different organization levels the factors would change, thus requiring the use of two or more systems. The various factors that commonly contain subfactors must be defined as accurately as possible. Points are frequently used to proportionally weight the relative values of the various factors. Then, job contents, on a factor-by-factor basis, are compared against the defined, standard compensable factors and usually accorded a point value or some other type of value. The total value of the factors determines the relative value of the job. The highest-value job is ranked number one, and all others are then ranked accordingly in descending value. In working with a factor-evaluation method, care must be exercised to properly weight the values of the factors and to avoid excessive overlap and duplication of factors. It's wise to avoid too much complexity, which makes the method difficult to understand and use, too costly to install and manage, and often in conflict with government laws and regulations.

While the primary responsibility for internal and external job evaluation should properly be assigned to the human resources function, management must participate in the process. In large organizations where the human resources function employs many specialists, the factor-evaluation methods are more likely to be used. In medium and small organizations where the human resources function employs few specialists, the primary responsibility for job evaluation usually rests with management. In such cases, the whole-job approach is usually best, because the human resources manager often does not have the time, expertise, or knowledge necessary to effectively employ a factor-type method. In such cases, the participation by key operations and other service or support-related managers is essential.

Managers who either currently have or want to avoid internal job-evaluation problems frequently employ consultants who specialize in compensation management. These consultants, who for the most part are qualified, often implement very complex and costly factor-evaluation-type systems. All too often, however, the people who will have to maintain the system after the consultants depart fail to do so. Either they never really understood what the consultants did or they find the system too cumbersome, time consuming, and costly to maintain.

Internal job evaluation often stimulates political gamesmanship among managers, and executive-level managers must take appropriate measures to minimize the game playing. The mere fact of knowing that executive-level managers will review the results of the process puts lower-level managers on notice that gamesmanship is unacceptable. Also, managers are often apprehensive or even fearful of internal job evaluation, because the process could result in significant changes in the compensation paid for jobs, leading to changes in specific managers' political influence. Additionally, changing what has historically existed in the relative value rankings of jobs will benefit some employees and hurt others. This re-ranking could cause adverse employee reactions. Major re-rankings of the relative value of jobs may have to be tempered by considerations of the potential seriousness of adverse reactions by employees.

In order for a job-evaluation program to work, it must be perceived as fair and equitable. Pressures exist to pay what jobs are worth relative to one another, and counterpressures exist to preserve historical compensation-differential relationships. The continued impact of technology on job content requires that managers periodically reevaluate the relative rankings of jobs. Any changes in relative rankings and the reasons for them must be carefully explained to employees. Employee participation in job evaluation as a means of reducing resistance must be approached with caution. Communication must be tempered by taking into account employees' ability to understand the reasoning behind decisions, especially those that are unpopular.

It is not necessary to evaluate every single job. Identifying what are called "benchmark" or "key" jobs is sufficient. They are ones that are representative of many others in the organization. Frequently, job content of various positions as shown on job descriptions will not be very different. If a few benchmark jobs are properly evaluated, others whose total value lies between the key positions can be easily ranked. "Grouped" jobs, whatever their particular organizational titles, happen to have about the same relative value to the organization.

The External Job-Evaluation Process

Because organizations have to compete for employees, existing or proposed levels of compensation for jobs must be compared with the compensation being offered by other organizations in the market for the same job skills. We refer to this comparison as external job evaluation. Just as is true for internal job evaluation, it is not necessary to evaluate all jobs.

Marketplace compensation information can be obtained by a variety of methods, including mailing questionnaires to other employers, attending professional meetings where compensation practices of various employers are discussed, and participating in and subscribing to surveys compiled and analyzed by third parties. Some surveys are limited to compensation for particular jobs, while others, such as the American Management Associations' surveys, cover a wide variety of jobs ranging from file clerk to chief executive officer.

The responsibility for obtaining and analyzing market information should be assigned to the human resources function. As in internal job evaluation, larger organizations usually have the trained personnel and available time to conduct this activity without the use of consultants. A smaller human resources function, depending on such factors as how much effort it wants to put into external job evaluation, should consider hiring consultants.

In using any external information, it is important that job contents be compared, since even though job titles may coincide, job content can and often does vary considerably from organization to organization. Sometimes an organization's job descriptions match exactly with surveyed organizations' job descriptions. More often, they do not. Job-content definitions for similarly titled jobs can even vary among surveys. Frequently, two or more job descriptions in a survey and corresponding compensation information have to be combined to correlate with the organization's job description.

When management uncovers significant differences in marketplace definitions for job content as compared with its own organization's definitions, a potentially serious problem exists. First is the fact that valid comparisons are more difficult to make, and second, and possibly more serious, is that employees misperceive what they should be paid. For example, suppose an employee has the job title "fleet manager" although the job consists of little more than record keeping and more appropriately should be titled something like "fleet records processor." The job holder may actually believe that he or she is a fleet manager and after comparing salary levels in different organizations may feel underpaid. This misconception will affect attitudes and could adversely affect job performance. A solution to the problem would be to change the job title. Changing job titles, however, should be approached with caution, because employees' feelings and social/political relationships may be adversely affected. The risks of damage have to be weighed against the costs of allowing misperceptions and misunderstandings to continue. There are no simple solutions for this problem.

External job evaluations can provide a useful check against internal evaluations. Discounting supply and demand for the moment, market data on compensation for a particular job might be significantly different when compared to the organization's internal relative ranking, possibly indicating that the internal evaluation of the job is incorrect. It could also mean that a shortage of applicants with the necessary training and experience has pushed salary levels beyond where they logically should be relative to what other people in jobs that have about the same relative worth are being paid. Because of competition for employees, the market cannot be ignored and will exert considerable influence on setting compensation levels. If management wants to attract and retain capable people, it must offer relatively competitive compensation.

An important question for managers to ask is, "In what labor market(s) are we competing for employees?" Historically, as a matter of accepted practice, insurance and banking organizations totally ignored geographic market information when establishing and reviewing compensation practices. It was a well-established practice to compare compensation practices only with other organizations in the same industry. This may be acceptable to employees whose skills are not transferable to different types of organizations. An insurance underwriter, for example, is not likely to find the same kind of work in a steel mill. However, people like accountants, industrial engineers, and human resources managers can apply their skills with relatively equal effectiveness in many different types of organizations.

Even the major employer in a particular locale cannot afford to ignore the market. Employees who believe that they are appreciably underpaid have a strong incentive to form or join a union to increase their compensation.

The appropriate market for potential employees varies with the nature of the organization's function, the kinds of skills it employs, the transferability of those skills, the mobility of people, and the travel time to work, as well as equal employment opportunity and affirmative action considerations and the influences of supply and demand. It is important to compare compensation practices with both the local labor market and the industry as a whole. For some jobs, particularly those where the supply of qualified people is limited or higher-level positions where employees tend to be more mobile, the scope of the labor market could be nationwide.

Attracting qualified people can be an expensive, time-consuming process; losing employees for salary reasons after they have been hired increases the costs. Money is only one reason why people accept, maintain, or terminate employment. But it is a very big reason. Employees generally compare their compensation on these bases:

How much am I paid relative to my expectations and needs?
How much am I paid relative to others doing different types of work who are employed by other organizations?
How much am I paid relative to others doing different types of work in this organization?
How much am I paid relative to others doing similar types of work in other organizations?
How much am I paid relative to others doing the same type of work in this organization?

Human resources has the primary responsibility to obtain information, analyze it, and present it to management for review so that correct decisions regarding compensation can be made. Internal and external job-evaluation data, including so-called fringe benefits, are needed by managers who want to establish a competitive compensation program. Management must provide the guidance and direction for human resources. Human resources, through analysis of the market, of the organization's success in attracting and retaining people, and of turnover, must keep management informed as to the compensation program's effectiveness in meeting defined objectives.

Developing Salary Structures

Without internal job ranking and external marketplace information, it is impossible to construct a competitive compensation program. Here again, the principal responsibility for gathering and analyzing information should reside with the human resources function. However, management must participate in developing both single and multiple structures, because policy decisions regarding compensation have to be made at all steps of the process. Some of the key policy decisions that must be made are:

How competitive do we want to be with the market?

How competitive can we afford to be?

Will our competitive position vary from job to job?

What other forms of compensation can we offer in addition to money?

How many salary structures should we have—one for all employees or separate ones for special groups of employees (clerical and technical, professional, trade, managerial, and so on)?

How many different grades, pay classes, or ranges should there be in the structure(s)?

How much overlap should exist between the various ranges, grades, or pay classes?

How much should we tell employees about our salary structure?

How are we going to treat employees whose salaries exceed the limit for their salary range?

How much salary progression should exist in the various ranges?

How do we treat employees whose salaries are below their range minimums?

On what criteria should salary progression within ranges occur—merit, seniority, a combination of both?

How do we determine the range for raises?

How often should employees be considered for raises?

How often should the salary structure be reviewed and, if necessary, revised or updated?

It would be inappropriate to allow the human resources function alone to dictate the answers to these important questions. Its role should be to provide input to the decision-making process. Because these decisions have a major impact on the entire organization, the most careful thought should go into making them. Once they have been made and put into practice, inconsistencies in their application or frequent major changes in their content should be avoided. As market and organizational conditions change, changes will, of course, have to be made. However, changes, as appropriate, should be made on a scheduled basis as part of an annual review process, not randomly. Minor adjustments are quite different from frequent major changes, which, especially if done randomly, may give employees the feeling that the program was not properly developed in the first place. Too many shifts in policy cause trust and confidence to erode.

Managers must remember that not everyone is going to agree with compensation policy decisions. Those who seriously disagree are likely to continually press for exceptions to be granted or for major policy changes. Executive management has the responsibility for controlling this sort of activity. A firm but tactful attitude is appropriate.

Once the market data is obtained, it must be analyzed and refined because (1) the information is usually dated as a result of the delay from the time it is gathered to the time it is published (up to one year is not uncommon); (2) variances in sample sizes and sampled organizations cause data bias; (3) data is presented in many different ways in surveys. The responsibility for data analysis should be assigned to human resources personnel. Data-analysis techniques may range from constructing simple histograms to plotting complex linear regressions. The objective of data analysis is to ensure that it accurately represents what exists in the market.

Figure 4.   Scatter diagram showing job clusters.

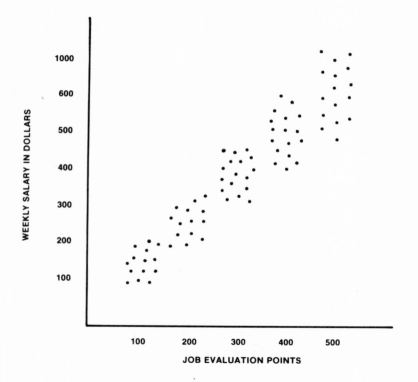

Figure 5. Scatter diagram with structured salary ranges.

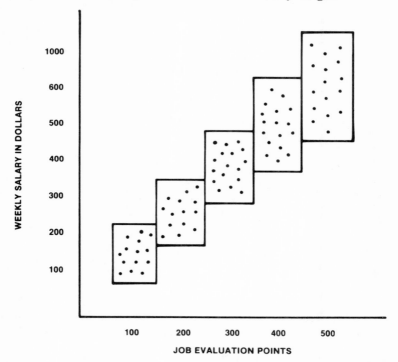

Internal and external job evaluations usually show that jobs, no matter what their specific titles, often exist in similar relative value groups. Each such group or cluster forms a nucleus for establishing salary ranges. Figure 4 shows job clusters based on internal job evaluation. Each dot on the graph represents a job or a number of jobs, their point value, and the corresponding salary. Graphically plotting all jobs or tabulating them shows internal ranking and salary. The number of salary ranges, pay classes, or grades, as they are often referred to, depends on the variance in job content among different jobs and the difference in compensation between the highest and lowest paid jobs. Figure 5 shows the

Figure 6.   Scatter diagram showing surveyed job market data.

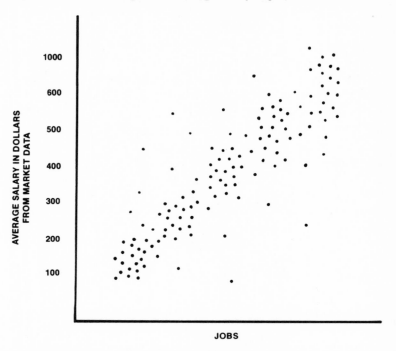

same information as Figure 4, but with ranges framed around existing jobs.

Although many different methods may be used to establish salary ranges, the end result should be the same, namely, to have all similarly valued jobs within the same minimum–maximum salary range. In establishing these ranges, consideration must be given to how they compare with the market, how much overlap exists between ranges (too much or too little can cause serious problems), and what the variance is between minimums and maximums to allow for career growth in salary. Again, too little or too much spread can cause serious problems.

Because of its complexity, the task of developing pay ranges should be assigned primarily to human resources with final approval coming from management. Before any structure is finalized, the figures must be compared with analyzed market data. Figure 6 shows graphically plotted market data for jobs comparable in content to key jobs in the organization.

Current rates of pay, specifically lowest, average, and highest for surveyed jobs, must be compared with what exists in the organization to determine how competitive the organization's salaries are with those paid in the market. But factors in addition to the market must be considered. One such important factor is the learning curve for jobs. Jobs with short time-span learning curves require less spread between minimums and maximums than jobs with long time-span learning curves.

Average experience levels must also be taken into consideration. For example, the market data may show that the average salary paid for information processors is $200 a week. If your organization's average is, say, $170 a week, it would appear that your organization is underpaying its employees. But let's say that 80 percent of the employees in the classification have been with your organization for less that two years, and it usually takes five years to develop proficiency in this kind of work. Because of the limited experience of your organization's employees, their average salaries should be lower than the average market salaries, if it is assumed that a relatively normal statistical distribution of experienced employees exists in the market.

Policy decisions regarding whether the organization desires to be a compensation leader, match the market, or follow the market must also be made. Based on this type of analysis, management can assess how competitive its salaries are. It should be noted that an organization does not have to pay the highest salaries to attract and retain competent, dedicated employees.

A particularly sensitive problem managers often have to cope with is what to do when employees are being paid at or over maximum for their salary range. Usually that comes about only with long-term employees. Human resources should provide information about the number of employees who are at or over maximums and how far over the maximum they are. Even though the employee is not responsible for the situation, the practice cannot be allowed to continue, because it undermines the credibility of the entire salary structure. One approach to this problem is to freeze employees' salaries until the range maximums move up to their level. We do not recommend this method though, because it can be seriously demoralizing. We believe it is more appropriate to gradually allow the range maximum to catch up to those employees by not giving them the full raise they may earn in a given year. This solution does not contradict the concept of merit. Employees must be told that they are over the maximum and to bring their salaries in line they must share part of the burden. Other solutions are available, but we believe this one to be the most practical.

Another problem often encountered by managers is what to do if the demand for certain job skills is so high that starting salaries have been pushed far higher than the point at which internal job evaluation shows they should be. A mistake that is commonly made is to move the position into a higher salary range in order to keep the salary being paid in line with the structure. This measure is usually a mistake. If the internal evaluation of the position was correct, then its relative ranking should not change. The position should remain in the appropriate pay range determined by the evaluation. The only effective way to handle this kind of problem in the short term is to allow starting salaries to move to where applicants can be attracted. To retain employees, salaries may have to rise above maximum. In time, supply usually reaches demand, and salaries may flatten out. This leveling occurred in the 1960s for engineers and is now affecting some jobs related to data processing. Human resources should be assigned the responsibility for carefully monitoring the kinds of situations described.

Assessing Performance

The area of compensation that is most difficult to manage is compensation based on performance. In fact, assessing or judging employee performance is one of the most difficult aspects of managing. Most organizations in the United States profess to use merit (that is, job performance) as the primary criterion for rewarding employees. In reality, most merit systems do not work out that way. It seems self-evident that because money is such a major influencer of job-related behavior, employees will adjust their behavior to acquire salary increases. Those managers who believe that salary increases should not be related to job performance fail to understand or do not want to accept the importance of money to most employees. In our opinion, employees should clearly understand that all forms of rewards, whether money, promotions, privileges, or status symbols, are directly related to their performance. If, in practice, rewards are given on bases other than job performance, employees' time and energy will be directed accordingly in order to gain the desired rewards.

Because most performance-assessment programs do not work as they should, managers often become frustrated to the point where they give the same percentage salary increases to virtually all employees. Exceptions are very rare. We disagree with this all-too-common practice. It takes a tremendous amount of time and energy to design, implement, and manage an effective performance-assessment program. But if it is done correctly, the benefits of reduced costs and increased productivity will greatly exceed any development and maintenance costs. One major reason for the failure of most performance-assessment programs is that the systems are poorly designed. Some of the flaws in design are:

Use of wrong performance criteria.
Vague definitions of performance criteria.
Vague definitions of degrees of performance.
Failure to weight performance factors.

While most systems can stand to be improved, even a well-designed system can fail to function properly simply because people are what they are. Some of the human and environmental variables that frequently contribute to problems are:

Prejudices and biases of assessors.

Political gaming skills of employees.

Attitudes of management and employees toward performance assessment.

Political pressures to statistically skew assessments to the high or low side, or even to maintain a normal distribution.

Lack of training in how to assess performance.

Lack of absolute or relative measures of employee performance.

Absence of controls to curb approval of biased assessments.

Ineffectiveness of existing controls.

In our opinion, many of the common problems that undermine the process of performance assessment and ultimately diminish management's credibility can be avoided or corrected. To do this requires a joint effort by human resources and management. Considering the nation's persistent problem of lagging productivity, it would appear that much can be gained and little lost by making improvements in this area. Why have many organizations avoided confronting the issue? Many reasons have been offered, but in the long run we seem to be guilty of taking the path of least resistance.

Any performance-assessment program where all levels of managers do not fully support the concept of distributing rewards based on performance is destined to fall short of what is desirable. The philosophy of the people at the top of any organization should set the basic tone and pattern for the organization's operational behavior. It is management's responsibility to determine the bases on which performance should be assessed and the absolute or relative standards for assessing it. Many managers, especially those who manage nonrepetitive work, argue that standards for such work cannot be established. Granted, it is more difficult to develop standards for nonrepetitive than for repetitive work, but every manager has a perception of what constitutes good, average, or unacceptable job performance. This assessment is measured by standards that must exist in every manager's mind. These standards, whether absolute or relative, must be job related and expressed in writing. It is important that common standards for similar kinds of work be established, agreed upon, and consistently adhered to by all managers. Inconsistency of standards and inconsistency of their application in assessing employees' job performance erodes the credibility of any assessment program.

The bases on which performance can be assessed will vary among different types of jobs. For example, leadership ability would be an important performance factor for managers but most likely not for custodians. To accommodate this kind of diversity an organization could have two or more systems. It is doubtful that even the largest organization would ever need more than four systems. Common performance factors can usually be identified for all operative and service employees, technical and professional employees, supervisors and mid-level managers, and executives. No system or systems will be perfect, because not all jobs fit perfectly into a specific system. No magic number of systems exists, but both too few or too many will cause problems. The decision on the number of systems should be made jointly by human resources and management.

It is also important that performance factors be weighted; that is, some relative value or importance must be attached to each factor. The purposes of weighting are to help employees understand what areas of job performance are to be emphasized, and to ensure that managers are consistent in weighting the relative importance of factors.

The development of a performance-assessment program should be shared. As already discussed, management has the responsibility for developing performance factors, standards, and factor weightings, and human resources carries out the actual design of the performance-assessment format and forms.

As previously noted, even having a well-designed system is no guarantee that it will function as intended. In order to increase the effectiveness of a good system, a number of activities should be placed in operation. Managers at all levels must be thoroughly indoctrinated with the organization's philosophy regarding the bases for rewarding good performance. Human resources personnel should be the reinforcers of the organization's stated philosophy through comprehensive training. Lectures, role playing, case studies, and simulations should all be employed. Training in and of itself is insufficient. It must be established that learning has occurred and will be practiced.

Comprehensive record keeping correlating the distribution of employees' performance by organizational unit with their productivity will provide information, which, if properly analyzed, will show how well the assessment process is working. The responsibility for information gathering and analysis should be shared by management with human resources. Those managers who do not properly implement the organization's philosophy should be identified and, as appropriate, corrective action taken. Unless the managers who properly implement performance-assessment programs are rewarded and action is initiated to change the behavior of those who do not, the performance-asessment process will not achieve desired results.

Executive-level managers who support equal and prescribed percentage allocations of each organizational unit's budget for salary increases inadvertently contradict any philosophy of pay for performance. In allocating equal percentages, an implicit assumption is made that on balance the performance of all organizational units is the same. This approach is only slightly better than giving across-the-board raises. Allocation of money for raises should be distributed on the basis of overall unit performance as compared with some objective standards. The more productive units as compared to the performance measurement standards should be given a higher percentage of the general budget for raises as compared to other units whose performance is lower. If all units are performing at a superior level, then overall profits should be higher. This, of course, assumes that management decisions are able to influence profitability. If profits are higher, then a larger amount of money should be available for raises. A range for merit raises should be established. The range should vary from year to year depending on such factors as availability of funds, government wage guidelines, and inflation.

In the nonprofit and government organization, budgeted money that is not spent because of good management practices should, in part, be allocated for larger salary increases. In reality, this rarely happens. What does happen is that money which is not spent is taken away the following year. This practice is regrettable because it encourages inefficiency and leads to ineffectiveness. To a much lesser degree the same problem exists in profit-oriented organizations, especially those where meaningful competition in the marketplace does not exist.

Readers who manage in unionized organizations, where pay increases are typically stipulated by the provisions of a negotiated labor agreement unless an employee is being demoted, have undoubtedly concluded that performance assessment is not feasible in such an environment. We disagree with this viewpoint. All employees, whether or not they are represented by a union, need feedback. In the absence of it, they will provide their own. Affirmation must be given for good performance and corrective action for poor performance. Negotiated labor agreements, or what are commonly called contracts, do not restrict management from disciplining employees whose performance is below par. Peformance assessment is a process through which behavior can be reinforced or modified. While nonmonetary rewards may not have as much value to employees as money, management is relatively free to give nonfinancial rewards to good employees in the unionized organization.

Utilizing Human Resources to Manage Salary Compression

Largely as a result of inflation, the overall availability of people, and the high demand for certain kinds of job skills, starting salaries for new employees have been moving faster than average total annual increases for present employees. This situation has precipitated job hopping and stirred up employees' perceptions about the fairness of their compensation. It is frustrating for an employee with five years of service, who has been receiving average annual increases, to see a new employee start at or near the same salary he or she has finally achieved. Such conditions are commonplace and are referred to as salary compression. Human resources can be utilized to provide valuable assistance to management in helping to avoid or correct salary compression problems. In a large organization, maintenance of salary information in a computer is essential because manual record keeping and analysis is too time consuming, costly, and prone to error. With the development of low-cost mini- and micro-computers, it is cost effective for organizations with as few as 50 employees to maintain all human-resources-related information in a computer.

Human resources can track the movement of salaries relative to length of employees' service, quality of service, starting salaries for new employees, and changes in the market. Salary inequities should be corrected before, not after, problems arise. If management is unaware that inequities exist, then problems cannot be avoided. Preventing problems is far better than reacting to them after they have occurred. If affordable, larger percentage raises or special parity adjustments can both be used to avoid or resolve salary compression problems.

5

Getting Results from
Training and Development Programs

The training and development of employees is an activity of increasing concern to organizations. In this chapter we will explore not only the reasons underlying this concern, but what steps organizations can take to maximize their returns on the money and effort invested in training. While the activity is known by other terms, including "employee education," it is most commonly referred to as "employee training" and "employee development." The two activities are distinct but have a common objective.

Training is the imparting of factual knowledge and specific job-related skills that will increase a person's aptitudes, skills, and abilities to perform specific jobs. Training also includes helping a person to reach an accepted level of proficiency in the practice of these skills. Apprenticeships are a common form of training.

Development is the broadening of a person's knowledge, understanding, and attitude along with judgment, analytical powers, ability to make decisions, and similar general skills. Planning, leadership, and communications are just some of a wide variety of topics typically covered by development activities. Since both training and development assume that a person is lacking in some knowledge or skill relative to certain standards, their common objective is to raise the level of knowledge or skill to meet those standards. The term "education," as used throughout this chapter, is a more generalized reference to training and development.

Given the generally accepted premise that in today's society people are better educated or at least have been exposed to and passed through higher levels of educational institutions than previous generations, the logical question is why organizations find it necessary to engage in more and more training and development activities. The reasons are varied. Some are long standing, while others are of recent origin. Here are some of the more commonly accepted causes:

- Technology has rapidly and often dramatically altered the way organizations do business, thereby causing obsolescence of learned skills.
- Educational institutions have frequently failed to provide the knowledge and skills people need to function adequately in the business world.
- Education is becoming increasingly accepted as a valuable, lifelong process.
- Certain kinds of skills and knowledge can be taught more effectively in the organizational world, where theory can be readily put into practice.
- People's expectations of what organizations should do for them have expanded far beyond just the job, salary, and benefits.
- To remain competitive, organizations find training and development essential to maintain a flexible and adaptive work force.

Change has always been one of the most significant conditions organizations have to cope with. At various stages in history, change has been rapid and dramatic, as in the twentieth century. Indications are that substantial change will continue, if not accelerate, for the remainder of this century. As an example, the advances brought about by the computer have revolutionized the way organizations function. Some claim this is just the beginning.

Change impacts on every facet of operations. Of importance to our discussion is how it affects the jobs that managers are called on to supervise and, indeed, the very process of management itself. One thing is for certain, change is inevitable. The only realistic approach is to anticipate it, prepare for it, and become its partner.

In more stable times, the curricula offered by secondary and higher-learning institutions was, for the most part, adequate in preparing people to enter the work world. At the very least, it provided them with a reasonably broad framework within which they could integrate theory with reality. Today, many institutions are caught in a dilemma. The number of students following the traditional path from high school to college to the work world has declined because of the decreasing birth rate and because of skepticism regarding the value of a college education. Consequently, many institutions are offering traditional curricula to a shrinking market. Conversely, an increasing market consists of those people already in the work force or those who had once been in and are now reentering it, as in the case of housewives whose children no longer need their constant care. It is unfortunate not only for these people but for the institutions themselves that they have not been able to adapt curricula quickly enough to new market needs. Consequently, some institutions face financial disaster because of too few students, some people cannot qualify for certain highly skilled or professional jobs because of unavailable education resources, and some organizations' needs remain unfulfilled because too few applicants possess the job skills required to fill the vacancies.

In some instances, educational institutions fail to provide the appropriate education because organizations send mixed signals about what kind of educational training they want in applicants. Organizations often hire people with qualifications that are quite different from what they say they want. In this way, they compound the problem by leaving curriculum decisions entirely up to the academic community. Accordingly, institutions may produce graduates with highly specialized knowledge and skills, only to find that candidates with a broad general education are in demand.

While considerable criticism, with some justification, has been directed at educators for being out of touch with events in the organizational world, far too few organizations have developed cooperative programs that allow educators the opportunity to gain experience in the organizational environment. Additionally, they fail to send managers and professional people into the educational community to help shape curricula, teach, or provide similar assistance.

The quality of education appears to have suffered in recent years. Because of government affirmative action and similar mandates, institutions have been compelled to lower admissions and grading standards. While the worth of the intention behind these steps cannot be debated, neither can the end result be ignored: Some students who have passed through and graduated from institutions have often failed to learn adequately and are poorly equipped to enter the job market.

Just as people have come to realize that education is more and more necessary to cope with a changing world, so have they come to desire and value it. In the past, a high school diploma or, more recently, a college degree was considered satisfactory. This accent is changing. More and more, the most significant portion of the educational process takes place after high school, college, or even graduate school. Nowadays the learning people acquire before they enter the work world is often inadequate to successfully carry them through their working life, and so education is becoming a lifelong process. It is not so much a continuous process as one punctuated with periods of intensive training and retraining to keep up with the impact of technology.

In response to the growing need for lifelong education, a variety of technical and other such institutions offering specialized training have sprung up. Unfortunately, however, the problem of providing continuing education is far from resolved. The validity of the education offered by some of these institutions has not yet been fully tested, and in some cases, it is highly questionable. In other instances, as we have mentioned, traditional institutions have failed to develop the kinds of relationships with the work world that would best serve their own interests as well as those of the people who seek their services.

In the past, education was viewed as primarily the responsibility of institutions and was thought to take place most effectively in the classroom. Organizations were poorly equipped to offer alternatives. Only recently has this dependency on educational institutions lessened. Organizations have, by necessity, been forced to assume the additional role of educator. A few innovative organizations, which saw this role as an opportunity, have demonstrated the many distinct advantages of moving education into the workplace. In fact, some of the best training and development programs have originated, not in traditional institutions, but in the job setting.

There are many advantages to educating people in the organizational setting. The subject matter is more precisely geared to the mutual needs of the worker-student and the organization, and interest in the needs and ultimate success of the student is assured. Moreover, specialized, on-the-job assistance is readily available to the student. On-site education is convenient to the student and to the organization, and education by the organization helps to assure a smooth transition from learning to doing.

An organization's involvement in educating its employees is highly compatible with the expectations of today's employees. A few short years ago, education, whether offered internally or externally through tuition reimbursement, was viewed as a fringe benefit and an uncommon one at that. By the same token, yesterday's employees and employers were not concerned about continuing education. Indeed, some organizations that very early recognized the need for employee growth through education were compelled to offer incentives as an inducement to their employees.

At one time, employees questioned the motives underlying the offer by organizations to provide for such nonwork needs as education, but now employees seem to expect the organization to meet needs whose work-relatedness may be questioned. In all probability, as employees become more aware of the potential value of adult education, the expectation will increase.

Previously, employee education was viewed by many organizations as a questionable expense. Today, it is more apt to be seen as an investment in the organization's future. Competition for applicants with specialized skills, rapid changes in technology, a highly mobile work force, and other factors have caused organizations to recognize the fact that to remain strong and competitive they need continually educated employees.

Purpose of Training and Development

Any discussion of education would be incomplete without a brief comment on the learning process. Training and development are conveyors of knowledge. How much knowledge is actually received and acted on depends on the participants in the process. Since learning is internal and voluntary and occurs within the individual mind, even the best designed or best conducted training or development program cannot guarantee that learning will take place.

For organizations to justify committing large amounts of time and money to training and development, the purpose of the program should be well defined. Poorly planned or inefficiently executed training programs can waste resources that could be better allocated elsewhere. An ineffective program can frustrate its managers and employees and reduce the credibility of training as a valuable tool for the organization. While the appropriate training approaches and methodologies vary according to such factors as the size of the organization, the purposes of training and development do not. They can be stated as follows:

- To provide otherwise qualified candidates for employment with certain knowledge or skills to perform specialized jobs.
- To provide current employees with certain knowledge or skills to perform newly created jobs or jobs that have changed and thus avoid or reduce the obsolescence of employees.
- To improve the quality of output.
- To improve the quantity of output.
- To reduce or resolve work-related problems such as high production costs, waste, accidents, absenteeism, and turnover.
- To increase the utilization of those talents and abilities that are unique to each employee.

Owing to a variety of factors, an organization may not be able to obtain applicants who are properly qualified for the job. In times of low unemployment or scarcity of available applicants as in rural areas or smaller cities, an organization's choice of applicants may be highly restricted. Particularly in lower-level jobs, where it may not be economically feasible to relocate large numbers of people, the only appropriate course of action is to train people in the specific job-related skills.

Equal employment opportunity and affirmative action laws have also prodded organizations into training newly hired employees. To meet hiring quotas for minorities and other so-called disadvantaged groups, organizations have had to offer extensive training programs to teach these employees the necessary job skills and sometimes even basic life skills.

As technology enters the work world to an increasingly degree, organizations are faced with the tremendous challenge of training their employees to keep pace. In recent times, many lower-level or routine jobs have been eliminated by mechanization—robots have replaced certain assembly-line functions and computers perform computations and other time-consuming and tedious tasks previously performed by people. While the impact of technology is often more visible in lower-level jobs that involve considerable repetition, it has also had a considerable effect on higher-level technical and professional jobs. Unless organizations recognize these changes and prepare for them through employee training, they run the risk of unwittingly maintaining an obsolete work force.

In addition, few employees give their all to an organization without expecting a lot in return. Unlike workers in the Depression era, who were content just to have employment, today's employees do not need to rely on organizations for financial security. Through unemployment compensation and social welfare programs, people can exist in reasonable comfort for extended periods of time without working at a job. They expect much more than a job, an attractive salary, and good benefits. Employees are increasingly concerned about their own growth. When they work in organizations that are experiencing high growth, they want a share in it. In addition to the growth factor is the issue of people's identification with their work. Much of who we are and how we feel about ourselves centers on our work—what we do for a living. Consequently, employees strongly want and need to develop. More and more, they look to the organization for the means to grow through training and development, either by means of programs offered directly by the organization or with financial or other kinds of support from it.

Productivity

Both the quality and quantity of productivity are two major problems currently facing many organizations. Our country's competitive position in the world has slipped in recent years, as is typified by two prime examples, the auto manufacturing industry and the steel industry. We grant that the reasons for the current situation are varied and complex; the fact is nonetheless that training could be used to help employees acquire the skills needed to remain productive and has not been. Because of the high cost of change and restrictive negotiated labor agreements, both management and employees, for their own reasons, have often either refused to change or have met the need to change reluctantly. Also, tighter government regulation has reduced the flexibility of organizations to adapt to changing conditions. Consequently, production costs continue to soar, while productivity continues to decline. In addition to training, employee development, as a distinct approach, can be used. As explained earlier in this chapter, employee development is aimed at broadening a person's knowledge, understanding, and attitude.

Productivity in the United States has declined because organizations and employees have allowed self-interest to get in the way. In addition to the drop in productivity, a lessening in the quality of what we produce gives ample proof of this statement. Where once our country was synonymous with high quality, we are now all too often known for faulty products. Other countries are becoming more advanced in the use of technology than our own. While we may also possess the technology, they are quicker to utilize what they have. As an example, compare the electronics industry in our country versus that of Japan.

Beyond the quantity and quality of productivity is the issue of the process by which productivity takes place. Such factors as high costs, waste, employee work-related accidents, absenteeism, and turnover have pushed production costs to such heights in some organizations as to threaten their existence. Regardless of how mechanized or sophisticated an operation is, employees are still an integral and highly important part of the process. Organizations that focus on the development of their technology without also focusing on the development of their employees are doomed to experience serious problems. Such problems alone are not the cause of high production costs; more accurately, they are the effect or end result of something more basic occurring within the organization.

The purpose of training and development, then, is specific and valid. Organizations can no longer afford to view these functions as either luxury items or activities of questionable value. Just as organizations spend money to keep computers, machines, and other mechanical equipment running smoothly, they must also spend money to ensure that their most valuable asset, their employees, can function as a major contributing part of the organization.

Critical Role of Managers

Up to now, discussion has centered on the purpose of employee training and development and its value to the organization. Organizations, however, are not amorphous or abstract entities. They are highly specific and personal communities comprising people with various talents, ideally, working together for their mutual benefit. Organizations do not operate by themselves. Somebody must shape them, give them purpose and direction, and make sure that the purpose and direction are carried out. This somebody is the manager. Regardless of the title or level, the essence of the managerial role can be summarized as follows: Management is the process of accomplishing results through people.

While it is not our intent to explore the management process or managers' responsibilities, we will point out here, since it is relevant, that a very basic responsibility is concern for the professional growth and development of their employees. Neither managers nor organizations can expect to grow if their employees do not also grow. This growth can be brought about by indirect and direct means.

Indirectly, managers can facilitate the growth of their employees by developing a job environment in which growth is encouraged. Many factors shape the job environment, the principal one being the importance managers attach to their people. Is the main interest really productivity itself? Shouldn't it be, rather, the process by which productivity takes place? The effectiveness of that process, as judged by the end result, is directly related to how managers treat employees. Frequently, managers have mixed priorities as to who or what comes first. In fact, however, higher levels of productivity and the associated lower costs are most likely to be achieved by managers who show a sincere interest in their employees' welfare.

It is a fact of organizational life that employees cannot be fooled or ignored, at least not for long. Managers who fail to recognize this truth are bound for difficulty, as are their organizations. While some managers nominally subscribe to this philosophy, their actions speak otherwise. Employees cannot be fooled into believing that an organization has their interests at heart if it does not. Nor, if ignored, will they perform at expected levels. If employees are convinced, however, that their managers are actively concerned with their growth, they are more likely to produce according to their abilities and organizations are more likely to reap the benefits of high productivity. Indirectly, managers can encourage their employees to grow by listening to them, being available to answer their questions, keeping them well informed, and counseling and guiding them.

The sum total of these and similar activities is that a productive working relationship begins to emerge, founded on mutual trust, confidence, and respect. These three factors cannot be commanded by anyone from anyone. They must be earned through what is a continual process. Trust, confidence, and respect are not easy to win and, by comparison, are easy to lose. Once lost, they are very difficult to regain. Just as managers want to win the respect, trust, and confidence of their employees, so must they be willing to give the same. This is what is meant by learning to view employees as individuals.

The direct means of helping employees to grow on the job is through training and development. Employees are limited as to how much they can train or develop themselves, at least in a way that is harmonious with the organization's needs. Whereas learning is an internal process, training and development imply external guidance and support, which must come from managers. If managers embrace the attitudes discussed here, the guidance and support will be given willingly. Conversely, if managers have an adverse view of training and development, the support will be missing.

As in every other aspect of the employer-employee relationship, the critical link is the manager. Employees who desire growth have few immediate alternatives that would benefit the organization if their managers fail in this crucial role. While employees can obtain training independently, the organization usually will not benefit and may actually lose. If employees perceive a lack of interest on the part of the organization, their likelihood of leaving increases. Training obtained on their own may be in preparation for a job change.

In other words, training and development programs benefit both the organization and its employees, and management's support of such programs is essential. The latter concept is extremely important. Indeed, professional growth within the organization is significantly influenced by the degree to which managers approve, encourage, and support employees' efforts. While employee training and development is a process that begins with orientation, it never ends until employees retire or otherwise leave the organization. The professional growth of employees is at the heart of the manager's job. In fact, it is difficult to imagine why managers would not be concerned with the growth of their employees, if for no other reason than to increase their own effectiveness.

As will be discussed in the following sections, the role of human resources is one of staff guidance and support to managers. If managers perform their role well in this area human resources need not and should not interfere. Even if human resources has to intercede, it should only be temporarily, until the situation has been resolved.

An Approach to Training and Development

Perhaps the reason training and development is not more readily embraced by managers is because the process is often misunderstood. Some managers view it as complex. In larger organizations, it can be both complex and comprehensive, principally because of the need for specialized training methodologies, large training staffs, and other support systems.

However, a basic approach to employee education can be formulated. It varies little. What does vary is the level of sophistication in utilizing the approach, depending on the size of the organization and the resources available to it. Even in the smallest organization, it can be used to attain results. The approach is, basically, recognizing that throughout the process managers are the key factor. They are the catalysts that make things happen and that keep the process going. Human resources provides many of the tools and supports that managers need. Together they form a partnership aimed at helping employees, increasing the effectiveness of managers, and in the long run strengthening the organization. Figure 7 illustrates the process.

Needs Assessment

As in any program, the approach to training and development begins with a thorough needs assessment. This step is perhaps the most critical. Unless needs are carefully identified, reasonably understood, and agreed on by the participants, any approach to addressing them is bound to be inefficient and misunderstood. Not only will the end results suffer, but the process will as well. If good results are not achieved, both managers and employees will be frustrated and the credibility of training and development lessened, thus making it difficult for future efforts to succeed. This situation also serves to reinforce the feelings of those managers who questioned the worth of any such effort to begin with and even dampens the enthusiasm of managers who genuinely believe in it.

Figure 7. A basic approach to training and development.

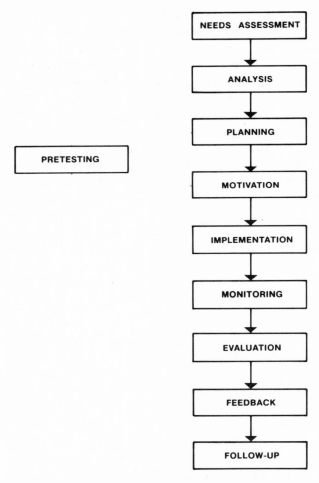

To illustrate the training and development process, examples of training to solve specific problems will be used. It is important to recognize, however, that training and development, as their purpose was previously outlined, have a broad range of applications, among them training new employees and existing employees as called for by job changes or advancement. Employee education should not be limited to resolving problems. Such a view is myopic and feeds the all-too-popular reactionary approach. Reactionary thinking fails to uncover the many and varied opportunities revealed by proactive thinking.

By virtue of their role, managers are in the best position to identify the training needs of their employees. Through on-the-job counseling and guidance, performance assessment, and other positive day-to-day involvement with employees, managers should have a firm grasp of their employees' talents and abilities and of how well they are being utilized. As will be discussed later, managers have many opportunities to motivate employees toward making full use of their potential.

Certain situations involving employees can be handled by the manager-employee relationship itself, such as the use of day-to-day informal counseling and guidance to solve problems. Other situations may call for more extensive treatment. A general principle applying to any action taken with respect to employees is to carefully identify the problem and plan the response before implementing the action. The first step, then, is to conduct a needs assessment, which is not as formidable as it sounds. To reiterate, managers should identify the problem or need. Care should be exercised not to confuse the cause of the problem with the effect. As an example, a manager has to determine if absenteeism is the real problem or the end result of something else troubling the organization. Managers should look beyond superficial conclusions. They must also avoid the pitfall of ending the needs assessment after only one cause of the problem has been identified. Frequently, a problem has more than one cause. The causes simply vary in their degree of influence on the problem. Not only is it essential that as many of the causes be identified as is possible, but how much influence each has must be understood so that action can be directed first toward the primary causes. The end result of this step is to formulate in specific terms a statement identifying what the needs are.

Analysis

In the next step, the statement of needs is analyzed, which involves asking questions to decide how to resolve the problem or address the needs. As these questions apply to the training and development process, they include the following:

Is training the answer?
Is it the only answer or just part of it?
Is it the best answer?
Is it feasible?

In seeking the answers to these questions, managers will want to call on human resources people. The value of their involvement is threefold: first, they provide managers with an objective view of the situation; second, they may have dealt with a similar situation elsewhere in the organization and be able to apply that experience to the current situation; finally, depending on the organization's size and that of human resources, they may have the expertise readily available to provide assistance. At the very least, as with the smaller human resources staff, they should know where to seek the outside help of consultants.

Sometimes training is not the answer; rather it is used to avoid coming to grips with the actual problem in hopes that it will disappear. Under such circumstances, training is bound to fail. In fact, it may serve to aggravate the problem. If training is the answer, it must be ascertained whether the other support mechanisms are needed. Frequently, training is only part of the answer. For example, in the case of unsatisfactory quality of output, trying to improve employees' skills may not be enough to resolve the problem. Other causes such as poor motivation or employee dissatisfaction may mean taking additional action.

Last, the question must be asked whether training is feasible. Feasibility is usually evaluated in terms of cost. The manager must decide if the end result justifies the cost. Costs are of four types: initial and ongoing; direct and indirect. Initial costs are those typically associated with the start-up process. They range from costs of planning to the costs of purchasing course material and equipment, of hiring staff if necessary, and of similar items early on. Ongoing costs include the maintenance of whatever effort was created, such as costs of updating course material and acquiring new material and equipment.

Direct costs are those that are up front and easily measurable, such as the dollar outlay to purchase equipment and hire staff. Indirect costs include such expenses as lost production time during an employee's training or while an employee is studying on the organization's time. Although less visible, these expenses are equally important. Regardless of how limited the training and development effort, it is costly to any organization. This factor is all the more reason for carefully defining the role of training in resolving a problem or addressing a need. It is especially important to establish the results expected. Conversely, the question must also be asked as to how costly it would be for the organization not to train its employees. Absenteeism, labor unrest, and high turnover are extremely costly.

Planning

Assuming that, after a thorough analysis, training is the appropriate solution and is feasible, the next step is planning. After needs assessment, planning is the most critical activity in the training and development process. It is the foundation of the process, and results achieved are in direct proportion to the thought and care given at this stage. Planning involves establishing training objectives, deciding who does what, determining the methodology that will be used, and similar important decisions. It requires considerable patience and thought. Planning can and usually does involve considerable cost to the organization, and some managers have difficulty justifying both the cost and the effort expended because they fail to grasp the meaning and importance of this step.

Whereas managers played a key role in the needs-assessment step, planning is a responsibility shared with human resources. In fact, human resources has the greater responsibility, since much of the activity is staff oriented. Also, by virtue of its overall role in the organization, human resources should have developed the appropriate experience, or at the very least have the knowledge necessary to ensure a successful planning effort. However, as in every step of the process, managers should never become separated from direct involvement. Even when certain aspects of the process are conducted primarily by human resources, managers should be kept informed and not hesitate to give their input.

The focal point of planning is defining the training objectives— what is intended to be accomplished by the training effort. In setting down these objectives, philosophical or abstract wording should be avoided. A well-expressed training objective is one that is to the point and written in language that all participants, including the students, can easily understand. This is essential for two key reasons. First, all participants much understand what is to be accomplished, and second, what is finally accomplished must be measurable. As mentioned earlier, learning is an internal process, taking place in the student's mind. The measure of whether the training objective has been achieved, therefore, is what the students do with what they have learned. This is observed through job performance—by how students apply their new skills to the job. At the outset, then, both management and human resources must agree on the training objective.

Following agreement, a variety of decisions need to be made on who does what, how, and when. The first decision concerns who does the training. In larger organizations, which usually have well-developed staff functions that include a training staff as part of their human resources operation, training can be most economically and expeditiously done by it. Smaller organizations, which typically do not have expertise in training, may require the assistance of outside consultants. Each approach has its advantages and disadvantages. The advantages of having in-house staff perform the training include control of the program material, ready availability of the time commitment needed, familiarity with the organization and work environment, and similar factors. Among the disadvantages are the costs associated with maintaining a training function and the necessary staff and equipment and the possible lack of expertise in either the latest techniques or specialized knowledge.

The use of consultants affords an organization objectivity in viewing its training needs and provides accessibility to a broader perspective than that of just the one organization. Larger organizations may also seek the services of consultants to train their personnel in controversial or sensitive areas, as, for example, in the management development efforts brought about by organizational change. As is true of all outside assistance, be it legal, financial, or otherwise, great care must be exercised in screening consultants for their expertise in the required subject matter and for their reliability. Human resources conducts the search for consultants, checks their credentials, and defines their working relationship with the organization.

Whether to devise material for the training effort or to obtain ready-made courses marketed by a variety of sources depends on how unique the organization's training needs and objectives are. Since devising training material is both costly and time consuming, obtaining ready-made material can substantially reduce costs and allow the organization to begin its effort more quickly. A considerable amount of good, if not excellent, material is available from highly reputable sources on many topics. Care should be taken, however, in selecting what is deemed appropriate material. On the one hand, ready-made material, understandably, is aimed at as wide a market as possible, so it cannot be effective in all situations. On the other hand, pride of authorship runs high among some internal training staffs, and managers would do well to guard against having training staffs reinvent the wheel by producing material that is readily available on the market.

Whether the material is chosen or developed, the roles of managers and human resources, particularly the training staff, must be thoroughly understood and mutually acknowledged. The training staff should be well versed in training methods, but they need not be experts in the material to be taught. Conversely, managers should not be expected to know training methods. Their role is to share with human resources the knowledge needed to construct the training material. Rarely are managers, who are experts in their respective fields, effective trainers. Since their knowledge of the subject matter is so thorough, they may have difficulty in being objective about what is important to impart to students.

Although excellent material may have been chosen or prepared for the training effort, that by itself does not guarantee success. To increase the likelihood that the students will receive the intended information, considerable care must be taken in planning how to conduct the training. While much of this activity is staff oriented, managers, because they have vested interest in the results, should be familiar with it. One consideration is where the training will be held. In larger organizations, where appropriate training facilities are likely to exist, there is little need to search for off-site facilities. Off-site training facilities may be useful, however, for such highly specialized efforts as management development where it is desirable to remove the students completely from their work environment. Of primary importance in choosing a location to conduct any kind of training, whether on the organization's premises or off-site, is that it be in an area reasonably removed from the student's normal work area to reduce interference and interruptions.

In planning for presentation of the material, thought should be given to the selection of appropriate audiovisual equipment. The use of such equipment has grown dramatically in recent years, owing principally to the powerful impact of television. Today's generations are more influenced by the spoken and visually portrayed word than by the written word. An indication of this influence is seen in the general decline in writing skills. To be effective, however, the audiovisual equipment must be used skillfully. Otherwise it can detract from the training effort.

Last, the question of who is to give the training should be carefully considered. As commented earlier, instructors need not be experts in the subject matter, but they do need to be very knowledgeable, and preferably experienced, in instructional methods. In presenting the training material, instructors become the key factor. Beyond the primary function of teaching, instructors have an additional and important responsibility: to give feedback on the students' classroom progress to both the managers and the human resources staff. Feedback is also essential from managers to the instructors and then back to the students. By becoming aware of those areas of the students' job performance that require improvement, as discussed with managers, the instructors are able to guide the students accordingly.

Pretesting

Before beginning the actual instruction portion of the training, some organizations prefer to pretest the employees who are to participate. The purpose of pretesting is twofold. It serves to measure how much students know or, conversely, where their knowledge is deficient. This information is valuable both in the final shaping of training material and instructional approaches and in guiding the instructors as to where to place the training emphasis. Pretesting also serves as a standard against which to measure post-training tests to determine how much the students have learned.

The use of testing is a function of the organization's philosophy and the subject being taught. In training that involves the learning of manual skills, for example, testing is superfluous since what students have learned can be readily observed and measured by how they apply it on their jobs. However, organizations should be cautious about regarding either pre- or post-training tests as an accurate means of assessing knowledge and learning acquired. If testing is used for this purpose, it should be done judiciously. This general principle applies to all testing.

Motivation

While motivation is an extremely broad topic, it does have a highly specific application and importance to training and development, or more precisely, to the learning process. It should also be recognized that managers have the primary responsibility to motivate their employees toward proper participation in training—the opportunity of instructors to motivate is restricted to their involvement with students during actual instruction. Motivation to training is like yeast to baking. In short, without it, little can be achieved.

As was discussed earlier, learning is an internal, voluntary process. Training may be forced on the individual but learning per se cannot be. Learning takes place most effectively when students understand the benefits to be gained, and the degree to which students understand the benefits is influenced by their managers.

Managers, by virtue of their position within the organization, also control many of the benefits, or rewards. The rewards to employees are of two types, extrinsic and intrinsic. Extrinsic rewards are characteristic of the employees' work environment. The relationship of extrinsic rewards to employees' behavior is relatively direct. Money is the most obvious extrinsic reward. Other examples are promotions, praise, recognition, affirmation, and similar benefits, although perhaps the most commonly used reward is money. Its lasting effect as a motivator, however, is limited. Unfortunately, many managers fail to use such equally effective rewards as affirmation and recognition. When given frequently and sincerely, their impact can be considerable. Unlike raises, they cost little to give, but when not given they can cost a great deal through problems caused by employees who are not motivated to learn.

Intrinsic rewards are inherent in the activity itself. The reward is the achievement of something. Examples include gaining knowledge or skill, self-respect, and similar forms of gratification derived from doing the job. Unlike extrinsic rewards, they cannot be controlled by managers or other external influences. Consequently, intrinsic rewards are often misunderstood by managers and, therefore, are rarely used as inducements to motivate employees.

This brings us to a fundamental issue. Do managers directly motivate employees? The answer is no. All people are motivated by nature toward one thing or another. Their behavior is influenced by their relationship with their environments of home, leisure, work, and the like. For purposes of our discussion, we are concerned with employees' relationships with their work environments. As was expressed earlier, managers have the primary responsibility to shape this environment. They do this principally through the use of extrinsic rewards. Through their responses to these rewards, employees, in essence, motivate themselves. Managers can increase their influence on motivation by learning to utilize more of the extrinsic rewards such as affirmation and recognition, and by tapping the sometimes largely unused intrinsic rewards.

Absent in this discussion has been the use of so-called negative stimuli, the principal one of which is discipline. Negative stimuli have limited effectiveness in the long term. Employees perceive little if any benefit in being guided by negative influences. With commitment already lacking, they will submit only as long as the perceived threat exists. Since work relationships are voluntary, employees will tolerate only so much before they eventually strike back.

To help assure successful training results that benefit both the employees and the organization, managers must make certain that employees understand why they are participating in the training effort and how it will benefit them. Equally important throughout training is managers' full support of their employees, demonstrated through affirmation and guidance.

Implementation
Much of the implementation activity is routine, if not mechanical. The range of the activity will vary depending on how extensive the training effort is, the type of training, whether it is to be conducted on one or several sites, as in the case of larger multilocation organizations, and similar considerations. Implementation in itself, however, can be a time-consuming effort.

Since much of the activity is staff oriented, human resources and its training staff typically assume the task of coordination, making certain that the various activities take place on schedule, and related responsibilities.

While management's role in this step of the process is not as extensive as it was in planning, it is nonetheless important. Again, by virtue of their vested interest in successful training results, managers will want to be familiar with, and kept informed about, each phase of implementation activity. Some managers may choose more direct involvement by participating in the opening training session. A few well-chosen preliminary remarks by managers can greatly help to set a positive tone for the effort and to assure the students of management's commitment.

Every precaution must be taken to ensure that a positive impression of the training effort is formed by each student. This is perhaps the most important part of the implementation process. If the training effort begins under a handicap of resistance or lack of enthusiasm resulting from negative impressions, it is very difficult to change those perceptions and the success of the effort becomes jeopardized. Assuming that proper planning has taken place, implementation of the plan should not be a difficult process.

Monitoring

Monitoring of the training effort occurs on two levels: the process of training and that of learning. Regarding training, it is human resources' responsibility to monitor and guide the overall effort and otherwise see that it is being conducted properly and according to schedule. With respect to whether the training effort produces learning by the student, human resources is responsible for measuring the process. Human resources should also keep managers posted on the progress of the total effort. Any changes in the program because of unforeseen circumstances should be reviewed with and, as required, approved by managers before implementation. By the same token, managers should not hesitate to share their perceptions with human resources, as gathered from observation or feedback from the students and other sources. Clearly, managers and human resources should keep each other fully informed so that no surprises occur in the combined effort.

This need for effective communication applies particularly to the learning process. Instructors should make it a number-one priority to advise managers of the students' progress. To be effective, this feedback should occur on a consistent basis, be objective, and relate each student's progress, or lack thereof, as compared to certain standards. Highly informal and subjective feedback is of little value and can even detract from the effort. It is particularly important in training, where classroom instruction is combined with practice on the job, for managers to give feedback to the instructors regarding the students' progress, using the same objectivity and other standards mentioned here.

Most organizations rely on observation as their main method of monitoring employees' progress. If tests or other formal measurement devices are used, their validity should be established. In addition, students should always be made aware of what is expected of them before they begin training. Introducing tests or any change in the program without first informing the students will reduce the credibility of management and the entire training effort and increase the likelihood of employee resistance.

Central to the monitoring process are the students. Feedback to them on their progress should be given consistently so that they can expect it at a particular time and use it as an additional means of gauging their progress. If a particular student's progress is insufficient or significant change is required in an employee's behavior, counseling should occur in a supportive manner. Who does it is not nearly so important as how it is done. Advice from neutral instructors is more likely to be viewed objectively by the students. On the other hand, counseling from managers has its advantages since it is the managers who control what rewards, such as salary increases and promotions, the employees will receive.

Evaluation

While a certain amount of evaluation is constantly taking place throughout the monitoring process, formal evaluation occurs at the completion of the instruction portion of the training effort. The entire training effort is not considered completed until formal feedback has been provided and the following steps have been fulfilled. This evaluation is the ultimate test of the appropriateness and effectiveness of the training effort. Its purpose is to ascertain the effectiveness of training in achieving the objectives outlined at the beginning of the program, and to determine the justification of the money, time, and effort spent in training.

To be effective, evaluation should be a structured process. It begins by both managers and human resources agreeing on what criteria will be used for evaluation. Various levels of criteria may be employed. The first level, commonly called immediate criteria, evaluates performance of the employee based on readily available data. It consists of test results or work samples. This information is then used to measure the effectiveness of training. This is the most commonly used and least costly level. Recognizing that no training or development effort produces a fully effective employee at its conclusion, second-level, or intermediate, criteria are sometimes employed. Critical to using intermediate criteria is knowing where to establish the arbitrary point in employees' progress after training at which they should be expected to have almost completely incorporated what they learned. The third level uses long-range criteria consisting of measuring training effectiveness in terms of employees' attitudes, attendance, and turnover. Criteria for this level are difficult to establish, and consequently organizations are reluctant to spend the money and effort to develop them. They do provide the ultimate test, though, by which to measure the effectiveness of the organization's overall training and development effort.

Whether only the first or all three levels are used is determined by how extensively and in what depth the organization desires to evaluate the training efforts. Even the use of all three levels does not guarantee the complete measurement of results. For example, assessing the level of learning of some topics typically taught in management development, such as effective communication, is difficult, if at all possible.

Based on the levels of criteria established, data is then obtained and measured against the criteria. Some interpretation may be required depending on the nature of the topic covered and the methodology used in the training effort. Evaluation is a staff-oriented activity usually performed by human resources. Not only should evaluation results be shared in depth with managers, but the methods for obtaining them as well.

Feedback

Feedback is the process of counseling employees on the overall progress in their learning and how they have applied that learning to their job responsibilities. It brings to a conclusion the formal portion of the training effort. Beyond discussing employees' training progress, the feedback step provides an opportunity for both managers and employees to assess career directions or, more specifically, what the next projected step in the employees' development might be. While the initial accent of the discussion is on advising employees of their progress, managers must be sensitive to listening to the employees' perceptions of their growth through training. Unless agreement between managers and employees is reached regarding what progress actually took place, each side will be operating solely on its own understanding, particularly in assessing what is requried in terms of future growth on the job.

Follow-up

This step is the final one in the training and development process, and the one that is never really quite completed. Follow-up consists of that activity which is routinely a part of the overall employer-employee relationship as developed and maintained by managers on a day-to-day basis. The emphasis at this stage is on maximum usage of what employees have learned through training. Since the work of the training staff has been completed, the opportunity of instructors for interaction with employees is limited. It is up to managers, then, to assure the success of this step. As will be discussed in the following section, one of the principal reasons for the failure of training is that managers have not given their full support, particularly to applying the newly acquired knowledge on the job.

Why Training and Development Efforts Fail

Whereas organizations are becoming increasingly interested in employee training and development, the results are frequently poor. Two principal reasons for less-than-desired results are that the organization, its managers, its employees, or all three do not have a clear understanding of the purpose of the effort, and that some or all three are not receptive to or supportive of the effort.

For any results-oriented activity to be effective for the participants, the activity's purpose and the benefits to be derived must be clearly understood by them. As this applies to training and developing employees, organizations through their managers must establish the purpose of the training. Managers have the responsibility to convey this purpose to the employees involved. If employees do not fully understand why they are being requested to participate in training, it is usually because managers have failed in the execution of this important responsibility. As mentioned previously, management is the key factor in achieving successful training results. This principle applies to all levels of management, including the chief executive officer. While executive management is not expected to know all the details of the training effort, it must understand its purpose and the benefits to be derived by both the organization and the employees.

In addition to understanding, full support must be given. Support begins with executive management, which shapes the organization's attitude toward the overall issue of employee growth and also determines what value is attached to the more specific issue of employee training and development. Beyond the organization's philosophy on employee growth, as expressed through such avenues as human resources policies, its attitude toward the development of employees is evidenced by unwritten policies and practices. Frequently, organizations espouse support of employee development through their written policies, but their actions speak otherwise. As examples,

- Executive management rarely rewards lower-level managers for carrying out effective employee training.
- Incongruities often exist between the organization's written philosophy on employee development and what it is prepared to do in terms of budgeting money for the effort.
- Executive management frequently stresses productivity to the extent that all other activity, such as training, is viewed as nonproductive and an interference with the productivity process.
- Executive management does not hold lower-level managers accountable for the development of their subordinates.

Even with the full support of executive management, successful training results are not ensured. Middle- and lower-level managers often do not support training, as evidenced by their practices, some of which are:

- After training, employees are discouraged by their managers from trying to implement on the job what they have learned because of the threat of change.
- Employee reward systems are based on short-term as opposed to long-term gains.
- Influenced by negative training experiences in their own career development, managers view employee training with mixed emotions, ranging from skepticism to overt refusal to lend support.

- Concerned with production schedules, managers often do not openly encourage their employees to participate in training.
- Managers may not have anticipated the training needs necessitated by changing jobs and the changing job environment until it is too late to allow for proper planning.
- Through improper selection, employees who do not have the ability or desire to grow may have been misplaced in training programs.
- Managers may be overtraining employees in relation to the present and projected future needs of their jobs.

Human resources people sometimes contribute to the failure of the organization's training efforts in these ways: They may not understand their role in the development of the organization's employees; they may lack the expertise to train and may not be aware of or willing to utilize the skills of consultants or other supportive services; they may have failed to monitor the organization's training needs.

Last, even though organizations and their managers have carefully exercised their responsibilities, training may still fail. If employees are reluctant to participate in training or do not motivate themselves to fulfill their responsibilities as active participants, no amount of external influence from organizations or managers will resolve the problem.

Successful training and development require the full support and active participation of the entire organization—executive management, human resources people, and managers and their subordinates. Each participant in the training process has a highly specific role and varying responsibilities, but all are bound together by one common objective, that of helping employees to grow with their organizations for their mutual benefit.

6

Using the Human Resources Function to Develop Productive Employee Relations

The continuing cooperation of employees is essential to any organization's ability to function well. In Chapter 1 we expressed our belief that all the activities of the human resources function pertain to either employment or employee relations. This is not to imply that employee relations is solely a human resources responsibility. Employee relations is a basic responsibility of all managers regardless of their other organizational responsibilities or hierarchical positions. Human resources' role in employee relations is to develop and maintain support systems that reinforce managers and facilitate cooperative relationships between employees and management. Over the long term, it is essential that good relations exist between the organization and its employees. When the employer-employee relationship fails, employee cooperation deteriorates and adversely affects organizational performance.

In recent years, considerable attention has been focused on employee relations. Attention is one thing; action that generates lasting, positive results is quite another. The failure of managers to develop and maintain productive employee relations is one of the principal reasons for the growth of unions and laws pertaining to fair-employment practices, labor relations, civil rights, and employee welfare and safety. So long as managers merely *speak* of developing productive employee relations but do not take action, unions and government will step in and in the process reduce management's authority and flexibility. Two choices are open to managers: either they develop productive employee relations or unions and government will do it for them.

The causes of problems in employee relations have many sources both in society and organizations. They have been attributed to the breakdown of the nuclear family, to the adverse influences of television, and to the collapse of discipline and learning in the schools. Much of what has been charged is valid. Managers frequently cite these conditions, over which they have little if any control, as the main reasons for poor employee relations. Considering the tendency of some managers to take the path of least resistance, it is easy to understand why they routinely transfer their problems, frustrations, and shortcomings elsewhere, rather than accept their share of the responsibility.

We believe that most employee-relations problems are caused by mismanagement and therefore are avoidable or correctable. Many managers lack foresight, and those who possess it rarely use it. They typically wait until after problems have developed before doing anything about them. Complacency and mediocrity in management are of epidemic proportions in many organizations. They are most acute where real competition in the marketplace does not exist. Good management that results in improved employee relations is an important way to reduce operational costs and increase productivity.

Why Managers Fail to Develop Productive Employee Relations

As we have stated throughout this book, most managers are reactive as opposed to proactive. It often requires a crisis such as a pending lawsuit, a pending EEO or other employee rights violation charge, an adverse decision or ruling from a government administrative agency or court of law, a union organizing campaign, a high rate of employee turnover, or pervasive employee absence and lateness to stimulate managers to take corrective action. In addition to being reactive, American managers, like Americans in general, are often impatient. They want instant solutions to complex problems and often call on experts to deliver the instant cure. Instant cures to complex problems are generally little more than superficial. The problem is resolved for the moment, and, one hopes, if everyone says enough prayers, it will not come back. However, as long as the causes still exist, the potential for the problem to reappear remains.

At least once every ten years or so, and even more frequently now because of the seriousness of productivity and employee-relations problems, new solutions to management's problems seem to appear from nowhere. The latest cures are employee stock-ownership plans and quality-control circles. The concepts of employee ownership and employee participation in decision making have been around for some time, but they are promoted as new ideas. Both have merits, but like many other cures that have surfaced, they will be oversold, misunderstood, improperly put into practice, and for the most part will not generate the results expected of them. Implementing solutions without understanding underlying causes is a hit-and-miss proposition that can result in even more problems.

Why is it that most managers talk about productive employee relations but do little to develop and maintain them? It certainly is not for a lack of information to guide their thinking. Considering the number of academic degrees granted by educational institutions over the past 20 years, especially the highly touted, over-rated MBA degree, as well as the proliferation of continuing education programs covering every facet of employee relations, the extent of the problem is incredible. Obviously, something is wrong. Strong arguments could be made that the difficulties stem from inferior quality in educational programs. We believe, however, that enough quality programs are available and, if carefully selected, can offer considerable instructive information. We see the problem as one of failing to put what is known into practice, not one of ignorance.

To differing degrees, all organizations are political environments where a variety of serious games are played. Because of this, managers, who usually have more to gain or lose than employees, must learn the rules of the game and how to play by them. The more political the environment, the more managers will adjust their behavior to acquire the organizational rewards they want and to avoid trouble. If one of the unwritten rules of the game is that candid discussions of problems are politically suicidal, managers learn to adjust their behavior accordingly. We refer to this behavior adjustment as learning how to "sing the organization's song." Managers who decide it is in their best interests to sing that song learn to say nothing or to say what others want to hear rather than risk being critical of the status quo and proposing a different course of action. Many organizations have nurtured this type of climate and found themselves in serious trouble.

Another cause of employee-relations problems is that most organizations gear their reward systems toward favoring short-term as opposed to long-term results. Short-term, results-oriented thinking at the top of an organization eventually filters down through all levels. The consequence is that any plans or programs which would produce negative short-term results before producing long-term payoffs are effectively discouraged. Decisions are made and programs implemented with little forethought to their long-term effects. What frequently results are short-term gains and long-term problems.

In order to survive and prosper in highly competitive markets where consumers have the ability to discern product or service differences, organizations must place a high emphasis on productivity and cost reduction. In their zeal to achieve and maintain high productivity at the lowest possible cost, they frequently give little more than lip service to employee relations. The prevailing attitude is that all this "human" or "employee relations" stuff is okay, but, "We have a business to operate and must maintain high production." Anything that diverts time, money, or other resources from production is frowned on. In such organizations, managers often hear that "People are the organization's most important resource" and that they must practice good employee relations—but see what happens if production slips a notch, or if one dollar more than what was budgeted is spent. Many managers who profess to be concerned about employees in reality often abuse and misuse them in order to achieve output and profit goals. Again, the result is short-term gains and long-term problems.

The present-day concern for people's rights in employment has brought about a proliferation of lawsuits, arbitrations, and all sorts of other claims and charges against organizations and individual managers. The result is that many managers are fearful of doing anything to upset employees. Often, because employees have easy access to internal or external due process mechanisms to seek redress for perceived injustices, many managers adopt a hands-off philosophy toward employee relations. This approach is just as dangerous as the aforementioned one, because in such a climate employees, if they choose to, can virtually do as they please without fear of being disciplined. Eventually, respect for management is eroded, leading to a loss of control.

The Employee-Relations Framework

Managers must recognize that productive employee relations do not evolve overnight. It takes time, patience, perseverance, energy, and money. Granted, in the short term, efforts to improve employee relations can adversely affect productivity and profits. However, in the long term, these efforts can encourage higher levels of cooperation resulting in lowered costs and increased productivity. Therefore, if management and all organizational support systems are oriented toward short-term performance, then a major realignment of thinking and major revisions in support systems are essential. But the necessity for changing policies, programs, and procedures to reflect a changing view of employee relations is frequently overlooked and explains why so many employee-relations efforts fail. It is something like trying to fit the proverbial square peg into the round hole.

Executive-level managers, in particular, must remember that they are responsible for developing a healthy organization that can survive over an extended period of time. If we ask people to make a commitment to the organization, the organization is obligated to make a reciprocal commitment. Common sense should lead us to recognize that when employees feel threatened they will respond in ways to protect themselves. History has shown that employees can develop very creative ways to do so and, if necessary, retaliate against those whom they perceive as threatening their welfare. Conversely, cooperation will be more readily given when employees feel secure and recognize that much of what they want from the organization can be gained by helping it achieve its goals.

It is vital that managers make employees understand that organizational rewards, regardless of their form, are given only as a result of cooperation. Rewards must be withheld when cooperation is absent. Managers must also remember that employees' cooperation is proportional to what they can gain or lose relative to what they want. Too many organizations, especially government, public utilities, and others whose ongoing existence is ensured, make the mistake of rewarding employees without requiring anything beyond a bare minimum in return. In our opinion, if employees can acquire the organizational rewards they want—money, status symbols, promotions, job security, and recognition—while giving no more than the minimum in return, most of them will behave accordingly. Why not? To do more would be a waste of time and energy.

If the employer-employee relationship is to be one of mutual exchange, then it must also be one of mutual benefit. What employers want from employees is relatively easy to define. Employers typically want employees to:

- Conduct themselves on the job in conformity with what is desired or expected.
- Maintain a high level of attendance and promptness in coming to work.
- Remain employed with the organization until at least the investment in the employee is recovered from services rendered.
- Produce the desired or expected quality and quantity of output.

What employees want or expect from the relationship with their employers is not always as easy to describe. Expectations and attitudes vary from person to person and are subject to change. Expectations are shaped by many factors, internal and external to the job environment. Unless managers understand what employees expect from the employment relationship, employee-relations policies, programs, and activities may be misdirected.

A vast amount of comprehensive research on employees' expectations and perceptions provides a solid base to guide organizations in developing improved employee relations. In general, employees expect from their employers:

Fair treatment.
Protection from abuse of power.
Adequate and equitable compensation.
Job security.
Opportunity to advance within their job or up the hierarchy.
Challenging and stimulating work.
Physically safe and reasonably comfortable work environment.
Feeling of being needed by the organization.

Recognition for contributions.
Adequate health and welfare benefits.
Psychologically safe and healthy work environment.
Sensitive, compassionate, and concerned supervisors.

To the extent possible, employee-relations practices should be sufficiently flexible to meet the needs of individual employees. In addition, because change occurs continuously, managers must periodically reassess existing employee-relations practices to be sure they are aligned with employee needs and expectations.

We believe that most people who voluntarily join organizations have accepted employment with the desire and intent of doing a fair day's work for a fair day's pay. However, these perceptions can vary widely from person to person. Managers and employees need a common, accepted understanding of them. Over time, the relationship between employers and employees will either strengthen or deteriorate. All too often the latter occurs. Typically, for some obvious and some not so obvious reasons, employees' commitment to their jobs often weakens, resulting in decreased productivity and efficiency. Managers may react with a variety of approaches, many of them negative.

A more favorable attitude, however, involves taking proactive instead of reactive steps to strengthen the relationship, thereby reducing the likelihood of serious problems. Minor difficulties, which are inevitable, can be effectively handled through existing mechanisms.

It is up to management to see that sound, productive employee-relations practices exist. Regardless of organizational size, human resources' role should be supportive and facilitative. First-level managers (supervisors), in particular, should continuously monitor the changing needs of employees and the adequacy of current practices. Support systems for upward communications should be devised by human resources and jointly maintained at all levels.

Designing and Maintaining Effective
Human Resources Policies

Managers are continually faced with the growth versus control dilemma. Simply stated, as organizations grow, management's ability to maintain control diminishes. High-speed travel, the computer, the telephone, and countless other inventions have enabled individual managers to maintain control over large organizations more readily than was possible in the past. One of the most pervasive and often most serious problems managers continually face is that of maintaining consistency in decision making regarding treatment of employees. The path of least resistance usually leads to treating all employees alike, which, of course, eliminates inconsistency and simplifies decision making. But unfortunately it also reduces the use of judgment, limits flexibility, and inhibits management development. Most seriously, such practices do not acknowledge the uniqueness of the employee or the merits of the situation. While in theory, treating all employees uniformly would seem to maintain consistency and fairness, in reality the opposite occurs. In fact, nothing could be more unfair than treating all employees alike.

However, if managers allowed one another to treat employees as they saw fit, inconsistency would surely occur. This, too, would result in perceived unfairness. It would appear that a "Catch 22" situation exists: treating employees alike and treating them differently both result in claims of unfairness. The solution lies somewhere in the middle. Most managers recognize that written policies are necessary to ensure continuity in applying the organization's philosophy to decision making. In the absence of written policy, no guide for decision making exists. Without guidance, lower-level managers will either defer or avoid making decisions, or, within reason, do as they please. Neither course is desirable.

Human resources policies are essential for an accepted

framework for decision making. They should be developed jointly by executive-level managers and human resources. Executive-level managers know what type of operational climate they want to maintain. Human resources has a dual responsibility. The first is to gather external information and analyze it for relevancy and usefulness. Such data would include:

Employment practices laws.
Government administrative agency decisions and awards.
Court decisions and awards.
Academic research pertaining to human behavior and em-
ployer-employee relations.
Trends in employment practices.
Trends in compensation and benefits.
Trends in union behavior and activities.

The second responsibility is to collect and analyze internally generated information. This information would include:

Turnover, absenteeism, and lateness data.
Frequency of and seriousness of employees' grievances,
gripes, and complaints.
Data on scrap and defects, complaints from customers, and
other quality-related information.
Quantity of work output relative to standards and expectations.
Job- and non-job-related accidents and illnesses.
Requests for transfers.
Raises and promotions.
Equal employment opportunity and affirmative action informa-
tion.
Unionization activities.
Where unions are present, information relating to level of coop-
eration or lack thereof.
Performance-assessment information.
Results of attitude or climate surveys.
Training activities.

Both the externally and internally generated information should be reviewed and analyzed on a continuing basis by human resources. If much of the information is maintained in an electronic data processing system, analysis can be accomplished more efficiently than if it is done manually. Data should be analyzed using descriptive as well as analytic statistical techniques. The results should be used to determine the adequacy of present policies, the need to maintain or revise them, and the need for new ones. All recommendations should be reviewed by executive-level managers before any action is taken.

Once again, the use of written policies that have guidelines for their application is stressed. Most large organizations have comprehensive human resources policy manuals. As most readers know, however, policies are often ignored or used only after a problem has developed, resulting in inconsistency in decision making and perceived unfairness by employees.

A number of reasons account for these common problems. In many instances, too many overlapping policies exist, or their technical or complex wording makes them difficult for most users to understand. As result, they are ignored. In addition, existing policies may be dated and no longer relevant to events in the work environment. Sometimes, policies are not available to the people who need them, particularly supervisors; or users, if they have access to the policies, do not know how to apply them to actual situations. Other reasons relate to managers who, under the guise of "maintaining flexibility," do not want controls placed on their authority and therefore disregard policies. Managers are often not rewarded for properly using policies or corrected when they misuse them. All these problems are correctable. Here are a few guidelines to avoid or resolve the most common ones:

- Write only those policies that are necessary. Some people attempt to justify their own existence and expand their scope of influence by generating unnecessary policies. The key question to ask is: Do we really need it?

- Write policies in plain and simple language. Avoid using examples, since their use often means that what has been written is not clear to the writer. As a result, it will not be clear to the reader.
- To the extent possible, ensure that policies are relevant to the situations that are likely to come up.
- Provide general guidelines for their application where appropriate.
- See to it that full support for their use is given directly by executive-level managers.
- Ensure that all levels of management who will use policies are fully trained in the logic underlying their formulation and application.
- Assign a copy of the policy manual to every employee with managerial responsibilities. This includes supervisors.
- Be sure that the policy manual is well organized with needed information readily accessible. It should include a table of contents, subject indexes, and color-coded sections. The more time managers have to spend searching for information, the less likely they will be to use the manual.
- Write some policies narrowly to ensure uniformity in decision making. Write others broadly to provide a general framework for decision making.
- Make sure that broadly written policies include guidelines for their usage.
- Enforce the principle that managers who do not follow policy must be denied rewards and corrected for their actions.

Human resources should be responsible for writing the final copy of approved policies and for ensuring that all levels of management learn to put them into practice. Failure to provide training in this skill is a major reason why policy manuals end up on a shelf gathering dust.

Properly designed and well-written policies that are adhered to by all levels of management increase the likelihood of consistency in the treatment of employees while providing sufficient flexibility for unique situations. In addition, employees are less likely to feel that management is unconcerned and treats them unfairly.

It is important that employees understand their employer's philosophy toward them. Communication of the organization's view begins during the employment process and should continue throughout the employment relationship. Many policies, programs, services, benefits, and opportunities designed to foster good employee relations are often unknown to the employees. During the orientation process, employees should be given an employee handbook reflecting the organization's philosophy and policies toward them. The handbook should focus on the employee, not superfluous procedural information.

Human resources should develop the employee handbook. Responsibility for reviewing its contents with newly hired employees should be shared with management, particularly with the immediate supervisors of new employees. It must be remembered, though, that an organization's credibility suffers if written words are not supported by action. Even the most positive attitudes can turn negative if reality differs significantly from stated policy. Employee handbooks are discussed in greater detail in Chapter 7.

Increasing the Frequency and Accuracy of Upward Communications

In most organizations communications usually flow down as opposed to up. But upward communications are equally important. Some of the benefits of a healthy flow of upward communications are:

Improved employee relations.
Development of a greater sense of belonging by employees.
Increase in employees' feelings of self-worth and confidence.

Opportunity for management to assess the quality of its leadership more accurately.

Access to useful information from employees to reduce costs,
increase productivity, resolve problems, capitalize on opportunities, and increase profits.

Upward communications may take a variety of forms including
suggestions, opinions, reactions, feelings, concerns, gripes, and
complaints. No matter what the form or how it is obtained, timely
and accurate information gleaned in this manner is essential to
organizational health. In most organizations, however, major ob-
stacles to upward communications exist, including the following:

Reluctance of employees to express their feelings and opinions
openly, because of concern about how it will be interpreted
and possible consequences.

Selective filtering and dilution of information as it passes
through various organizational levels.

The view held by employees that management is not interested
in what they have to say.

A similar view that no matter what they say, nothing is going to
change anyway.

Awareness on the part of employees that some managers want
to hear only things that reaffirm or reinforce what they are
already doing.

These conditions prevent information from reaching the people
who have the authority to make changes. Or it may reach them in
such a diluted or distorted form that it is useless.

In any communication, feedback is important. For one thing, it
helps management to determine if understanding exists and compliance can be expected. Without feedback, systems cannot make
adjustments that are vital to their functioning. Listening is also an
inherent part of the feedback process. It is a skill that managers
should practice.

When an organization has feedback problems, conditions often
do not change until they have become critical. If managers are

willing to invest the time and effort, this kind of situation is avoidable. Ways to increase the frequency and accuracy of employee feedback can be initiated by managers. It should also be remembered that not all information communicated upward has to be in the form of feedback. Management should also encourage employees to communicate their ideas, suggestions, and opinions.

Trust between employees and management is crucial. Employees are always aware that when they openly express their feelings and opinions, they are taking a risk. They may or may not trust their immediate supervisors. But if they do not trust those above them at successively higher levels, openness in communications will be reduced proportionately.

Meetings are often relied on to maintain two-way communications. However, they frequently fail to do so. For one thing, communications in meetings are usually downward. Some additional reasons meetings often fail are:

Objectives and agendas are unknown or poorly stated.
A feeling of distrust and lack of confidence dominates.
The wrong time or location has been chosen.
The number of participants is too large.
Hidden agendas and political gamesmanship interfere with constructive results.
Leadership is ineffective.
No opportunity for input or feedback is provided.
The physical environment is unsuitable.
The atmosphere is too structured and overcontrolled.
Too short a notice has been given to allow adequate time for preparation.

Rather than focusing on the ways in which managers can make better use of meetings, we choose to recommend that the situation be analyzed, the problem identified, and, as appropriate, corrective action taken.

In addition to meetings, other ways of facilitating upward communications can also be utilized. Human resources should play a key role in their development. Employee suggestion programs have been in use for some time and, if properly designed and administered, are a good means of upward communication. However, they are restricted to specific suggestions for improvements. Of more recent origin are "pipeline" or similarly named programs, which encompass opinions, general concerns, questions that cannot be answered by other means, and suggestions. Human resources should design and administer such a program, and higher-level management should participate by reviewing and responding to the pipeline information. The major reason suggestion programs often do not work is that managers neglect to take the time to respond to the input promptly and thoroughly. No matter how ridiculous an employee's inquiry or suggestion may seem, if the employee took the time to put it in writing and sign it, management should take the time to answer it. A system of progressive financial and nonfinancial awards should be established for suggestions that are used.

Human resources should formulate in writing the procedures to be followed, design the appropriate forms, do preliminary screening of the data, participate in the review process, and assist management in responding to employees. The review committee should comprise managers from various operating functions and should meet monthly.

As mentioned previously, in the past few years, quality-control circles have received much publicity. Many people erroneously believe that they started in Japan. This is incorrect. Quality-control circles, which allow employee participation in problem-solving techniques, originated in the United States, but as the Japanese have done so frequently, they made better use of what we developed. Programs for soliciting employee input on how to resolve problems can be practiced in any kind of organization. To work, the program requires a desire and willingness on the part of all levels of management, particularly the executive level. If it doesn't work, the reason can usually be traced to management's resistance toward allowing it to. Quality-control circles are discussed again in Chapter 7.

Another potentially useful upward-communications tool is the attitude survey. Management attitude surveys are largely unnecessary in organizations where all levels of management are well attuned to employees. Because managers often lose touch with their employees, however, the attitude survey can be useful. Its design and implementation and analysis of the results should be done by human resources. Approval of the final instrument prior to application should come from executive-level management. Because of the high level of skill required to design an unbiased instrument and the sophisticated statistical methods used for data analyses, bringing in consultants should be considered.

If an attitude survey is used, management must evaluate the results objectively and be willing to take action on matters of most concern. It is not uncommon for the results of attitude surveys to focus attention on deeply rooted problems that can often be attributed to individual managers. If executive-level management is unwilling to come to grips with such results and act on them, their credibility in the eyes of employees will suffer.

In our opinion every organization, whether its employees are members of a union or are nonunion, should have some form of employee-concern resolution. Such procedures, which in unionized organizations are called grievance procedures, are important upward-communications vehicles. They provide employees with some assurance that they will be able to seek redress to unfair treatment without fear of reprisals and without having to use external sources such as courts and government agencies. On occasion, even the best-intended actions by managers may cause unsought consequences. Until recently, managers have done a less than credible job in ensuring that employees' rights are protected and that adequate internal due process mechanisms work as designed. This condition has been a major factor influencing the growth of unions and the enactment of employee health and welfare legislation, especially legislation protecting employee rights.

For productive employee relations, management must be sure

that self-regulating controls are in place. When employees perceive that management will listen and respond objectively to their concerns and questions, they are less likely to appeal to outsiders for assistance.

Some organizations rely on an open-door policy for a grievance, concern, or complaint-handling procedure. The open-door policy is potentially risky for the following reasons:

- Higher-level management too frequently becomes involved in matters that could be handled by lower-level management.
- Time limits for responding often do not exist. Time delays may raise anxieties and expectations.
- Employees may misuse the system by circumventing their supervisors and taking their concerns directly "to the top." Such a practice is often at the expense of the relationship between employees and their immediate supervisors.

Human resources should design the grievance- or concern-handling program. Depending on the size of the organization and management's attitude toward the human resources function, the involvement of human resources in listening to and responding to employees' concerns will vary. Its role should be more one of offering advice and counsel as opposed to having the primary authority to settle grievances. However, when lower-level managers do not willingly modify their own decisions if they have been found to be in error, then human resources should have some measure of override authority, especially in cases where violation of policy is obvious.

Employee Services

Employee relations can also be strengthened by providing a variety of employee services. Which services are appropriate for any given organization should be decided by executive-level managers with input from human resources. These services should not be used to substitute for management's direct responsibility to employees. They should be viewed as support mechanisms to reinforce managers' main task, namely, strengthening employees' commitment to the organization and its goals.

Employee organizations in the form of clubs, leagues, or activity associations are easily established and can be partially or totally financed at minimal cost. While being in a bowling league will not contribute directly to increasing an employee's production or to reducing costs, it is a benefit the employee who joins will appreciate.

Employee-service awards in the form of pins, plaques, and letters of commendation all serve to recognize employees on some basis of merit or seniority. Such awards cost little and can be important in influencing attitudes. But employees must perceive that performance-recognition awards are given on merit and not for any other reason.

Job posting and bidding programs benefit employees and managers alike. They provide an opportunity for employees to grow professionally through promotion or horizontal job transfers. Over time and as people move through different phases, their aspirations, needs and wants, and values change. An employee may grow tired of a particular job and want to do something else. Organizations, like people, change. Methods, processes, structures, and jobs themselves all change as the organization struggles to survive by adapting to its environment. Flexible job posting and bidding programs, coupled with training, allow the organization to better utilize its employees, and employees to better satisfy their own changing work needs. Job posting and bidding programs are nothing new. Managers have long recognized their merits. However, they often fail to work as well as they should because:

Employees do not understand how the program works.
Employees who are not awarded promotions or transfers are too often not told the reasons, leaving the explanation to their imaginations.

Procedural guidelines with control mechanisms have not been developed and/or properly utilized.

Too often, managers do not follow policy and award jobs on bases other than merit.

The bottom line is that employee relations suffer when any of the above situations exist. However, these conditions can be avoided or at least minimized, and human resources can provide an important service to managers in this regard. First, a comprehensive policy with procedural guidelines should be written by human resources, subject to final approval from executive-level management. Once the program is approved, communication of it to all employees and training for managers should be assigned to human resources. Checks and balances must be in place so that the program operates as designed. Human resources' role can be limited to merely receiving recommendations or can be expanded to include direct involvement in the evaluation and feedback process. Human resources should participate in the investigation of any employee complaints that they have been unfairly evaluated. Recognition programs and job posting as tools to improve the employer-employee relationship are discussed further in Chapter 7.

An organization, especially one that is in the public eye or is a major employer in a particular geographic area, must be sensitive about its image. Studies show that an organization's image affects people's desire to seek, accept, and maintain employment with it. As we discussed in Chapter 2, people's perceptions of an organization may be formed even before they have formal contact with it. An organization that is positively involved in community activities is more likely to develop a favorable image than one that is not. Again, however, nothing substitutes for the feelings that employees take home with them from the job into the community.

It is especially important for organizations to develop good relations with sources of potential applicants. For example, as part of good relations with the educational community, we suggest that cooperative ventures with institutions of learning be considered, such as funded research, internships, scholarships, speaking to students, facility tours, and faculty-management exchange programs. Human resources can be in charge of contact and coordination for such activities.

Employee Assistance Programs

As employees have come to expect more from their employers, managements have become more aware of the benefits that can be derived from employee-assistance programs. However, an organization's ability to provide such programs is limited by the availability of personnel and financial resources.

All people at various times in their lives have problems that they find hard to deal with. These problems may be job- or non-job-related. When confronted with problems, people will eventually choose either constructive or destructive courses of action. Regardless of the origin of a problem, an employee who experiences difficulty in coping is far more likely to have the problem adversely affect job performance than one who copes successfully.

When an employee's performance does not measure up to expectations, both the employer and the employee suffer. If the employee becomes mentally or physically disabled, the employer will directly or indirectly pay the bills. It is far better, and in the long run more economical, for employers to try to help employees in trouble before their problems become serious.

In addition to the counseling that managers can routinely give, specialized employee-assistance programs should be available for the employee whose problem is more serious or who cannot talk with his or her supervisor. The employer who helps an employee overcome a problem will gain in the eyes of the employee and others who become aware of the organization's commitment to its members.

Providing specialized assistance for troubled employees should be assigned to human resources. In the small organization, where the human resources function is limited, liaisons should be developed with accessible social services and mental health professionals and organizations. A large organization can often justify the cost of having such professionals on the staff. Helping employees to remain healthy and productive members of the organization through employee-assistance programs is discussed further in Chapter 7.

Tuition Reimbursement and Scholarships

Tuition reimbursement and scholarship programs as employee benefits were virtually unheard of 40 years ago. Today, they are not only commonplace but are often expected by employees. Tuition reimbursement programs are relatively simple to establish and maintain and should be in the hands of human resources. Management, with guidance from human resources, must address the following questions:

Should reimbursement be offered for non-job-related courses?
What proportion of fees and related expenses should be reimbursed?
What is the maximum number of employees to whom we want to offer eligibility for reimbursement each year?
Should time off from work be given to attend classes?

In setting up a scholarship fund, the main task is establishing eligibility requirements and formulating the criteria and process for selecting recipients. Human resources should implement the program.

Career Counseling and Assessment Centers

Generally, employees are satisfied when they feel their skills are being put to use and are appreciated. However, attitude surveys and other upward communications tools reveal that employees often feel the opposite, resulting in poor employee-employer relations. Career counseling and assessment centers are only two of a number of techniques that should be available.

Career counseling should be carried out by managers, but human resources can be used to coordinate counseling across organizational-unit boundaries. Managers of various organizational units can provide counseling to groups or individuals about career opportunities and about specific job content. The information gathered from counseling should be maintained in a human resources information system so that when positions become available interested employees from anywhere in the organization can be considered. The use of career counseling as a tool to enhance the return on an organization's investment in its employees by promoting their growth is discussed in greater detail in Chapter 7.

Frequently, people do not have specific, long-term career goals. In addition, it is known that people perform at higher levels in jobs they enjoy. Assessment centers can be used to show employees, according to the results of tests, exercises, and interviews, what their aptitudes and interests are. Well-utilized employees are far more likely to be higher producers and less prone to absence and turnover than those who are not. Setting up and managing an assessment center should be handled by human resources. In the small organization, however, the expense of such a center is prohibitive and the outside services of organizations or individuals should be considered.

Relocation Programs

Virtually all organizations that hire or transfer employees from outside the organization's immediate geographic locale have relocation programs. The scope of such programs varies widely. Relocation can be a traumatic experience for an employee, and although most organizations do a credible job of handling financial matters, they often do a less-than-credible job with nonfinancial ones. Problems, both large and small, range from where to find a health-care professional to how and where to buy new auto license tags. All of them can be frustrating and time consuming.

For this reason, someone, or a number of different people, in either human resources or management, or possibly outsiders, should be assigned to assist relocated employees. Helping a spouse find a job or just getting to know his or her way around town, for example, could be crucial. As stated earlier, first impressions are enduring, and some difficulties can create long-term problems if not properly handled. If an employee's spouse becomes unhappy because of relocation problems, serious marital conflicts can result. Eventually the situation will affect employer-employee relations and job performance.

Preretirement Counseling

A fact we hope has become evident through this book is that organizations have been expanding the scope of their responsibilities to employees. Because at no other time in recent history have retirees faced more challenges and uncertainties than today, we feel that a preretirement counseling program is an important tool that can demonstrate to employees the organization's concern for their well-being even after employment terminates. The effect on employees' attitudes can only be positive. Preretirement programs as a tool to improve the employee-employer relationship are discussed further in Chapter 7.

Human resources should be in charge of any preretirement program and develop liaisons with various people who can speak authoritatively to pre- and even post-retirees about retirement. Particular attention should be directed to health care, financial management, and activity planning. The average age of employees is a major factor that will shape the program. If the organization has few employees approaching retirement, then the cost versus benefit of a comprehensive program would be questionable. The larger the number of potential retirees, the more comprehensive the program should be. Those employees near retirement will obviously see a greater benefit in such a program than younger employees, who are more concerned about opportunity and challenge as opposed to retirement.

An adjunct to preretirement counseling is a program that recruits retirees for a variety of part-time jobs. The cost savings to employers in not having to hire temporary personnel could be significant. Additionally, retired employees are often appreciative of the opportunity to stay busy and will certainly voice their appreciation to others.

7

A Review of Human Resources Tools and Techniques at Your Disposal

In the mid-1960s, American society entered a period of new awareness of the rights, needs, and desires of the individual. Previously, society had functioned on the basis of what was good for the majority. With few exceptions, individual interests were considered secondary. Respect for authority served as the foundation for this dedication to the common good.

This focus on the individual occurred suddenly, even though in retrospect the change that was coming and its reasons were both relatively apparent, but largely ignored. Some of the reasons were of recent origin, while others were long-standing. In part, they included the following:

• New generations had been raised on the premise that the want and deprivation their parents and grandparents had experienced during the Depression and World War II would not be repeated. As a result, their expectations of what society owed them greatly increased beyond what previous generations had expected or received.

• Parental permissiveness reached an all-time high. Again, to compensate for what they themselves had been denied because of difficult times, parents allowed their children considerably greater freedoms. Society, through such institutions as government, education, and even religion, supported this permissiveness. Accordingly, younger people soon to enter the work world developed a greatly diminished perception of what their personal responsibilities should be.

• The nation's economy was prosperous. People generally had enough money and leisure time to pursue personal interests, adding new dimensions to their lives. Employees' identities expanded beyond the workplace, and their reliance on the job environment for a sense of worth declined.

• The postwar baby boom was coming to an end—birth rates were dropping. Fewer people, especially those with the required education and skills, were available to fill the growing number of new jobs created by the prosperous economy. People often were very selective in accepting job offers and very demanding in what they expected. The importance of job security had dramatically decreased.

• With a new emphasis on education brought about largely by technological advances, people began to take greater advantage of educational opportunities. It was no longer uncommon to graduate from college. With increased exposure to education came increased expectations.

• Civil rights and similar legislation, supported by highly vocal groups in the population, forced society to recognize a greater and greater number of individual rights and freedoms. This movement had a tremendous effect on lessening people's reluctance to speak out on or question issues in every segment and institution of society.

As a result of these other factors, people came to place great value on their new-found freedoms. What emerged almost as a by-product of this change soon became a central issue, namely, "What role should externally imposed authority have in an individual's life?" Until the mid-1960s, people had generally accepted authority as a necessary and stabilizing force in their lives. In their quest for self-expression and personal fulfillment, people came to rely less on the kind of stability represented by authority.

Thus, the pendulum had swung from one extreme to the other. As people's dependence on authority decreased, they began to question it more and more, and then eventually challenge it. At the height of the movement, which started in the mid-1960s, people openly provoked and often defied authority in nearly every aspect of society. Not only was the authority of governments, businesses, and industries suspect, but so was that of many other social institutions, such as religious and charitable organizations, which had traditionally enjoyed almost unquestioning public support. Whereas some of the issues were the same as those raised by previous generations, the generation of the sixties was less hesitant to speak out.

At the movement's height, rebellion against authority seemed indiscriminate. Often the objective was simply to challenge—the reason was of secondary, if indeed of any, importance. Also, little effort was made to propose alternatives to what was being attacked.

It proved to be a difficult time for many organizations. The need to exercise authority had always been essential to effective management, and it had worked comparatively well for many years. Times were prosperous. Employees were far better off than previous generations had been in terms of compensation, opportunities, working conditions, job security, and leisure time. Consequently, some organizations saw what was happening as a threat and reacted by attempting to reinforce their control over employees. Other organizations viewed events with mixed emotions, ranging from frustration to helplessness, and seemingly did not know how to respond but merely hoped that it would all soon go away. A few organizations quickly grasped the significance of the movement and found new ways to bring employees into closer harmony with the organization.

The tremendous impact of this movement on society, its value systems, and expectations, is now a matter of history. It would be absurd to believe that we could return to the conditions of the pre-1960 era. The only feasible conclusion seems clear. Employees expect a greater voice in organizations, and this fact of organizational life has to be accepted.

The task, then, is to find significant ways to involve employees in their organizations for mutual benefit. Some managers will see this course as an abrogation of managerial prerogatives. It need not be. As discussed previously, employees represent a vast resource of creativity largely untapped by many organizations. In this context, the management process can become one of rediscovering and utilizing this resource.

The purpose of this chapter is to present various tools and techniques—both traditional and new—that will facilitate this process. Like most tools, they are valuable only if understood and properly used. While in many organizations some are used primarily by the human resources function, the underlying principles can be applied by managers to achieve the same results. In any event, managers should be familiar with them since both management and human resources share the common objective of drawing on the best in their employees. For convenience of discussion, the tools and techniques may be divided into the categories shown in Figure 8.

Considerable overlap can exist among the tools depending on how they are employed, the organizational setting, and similar variables. Regardless of the specific tool, however, or how it is used, all share the common purpose of promoting the better assimilation of employees into the organization.

Employee-Input Tools and Techniques

In general, it is unrealistic to expect a person to feel commitment to an activity without having a vested interest in it. It is basic to human behavior to want what may be termed "ownership," or identification, with the end result. As this applies to employees

Figure 8. Tools and techniques to assimilate the employee into the organization.

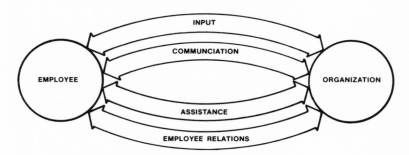

functioning in organizations, it is no longer a matter of merely acknowledging that employees *want* involvement; it is essential to recognize their *need* to be involved. Lest the subtlety of this difference be overlooked, it is well to remember that work occupies a major portion of people's lives. Accordingly, people's identities are often largely shaped by not only what they do, but how well they do it. As discussed earlier, studies demonstrate that people need to be competent in their work-related activity and to be recognized for it.

However, allowing employee involvement or influence is often seen by organizations as giving up control. Organizations are, of course, controlled environments. Employees and managers at all levels must accept a certain degree of control over their activities, which is not necessarily a negative thing; rather it is crucial to running organizations. How to exercise that control for the good of an organization and its employees is the challenge facing management.

As the issue of control applies to employee involvement, many organizations find themselves in a dilemma. But for organizations to equate employee involvement with relinquishing control is often erroneous. In fact, employee involvement can actually reduce the need for control in some areas and allow management to better direct its efforts toward other aspects of the organization's operation.

Perhaps the best illustration of this point is management's reluctance to capitalize on employee input. The fear is that employees will not confine their input to the particular issue under consideration. In addition, many managers who feel they must provide all the answers fear they will be looked on unfavorably by both employees and higher-level managers if some solutions to problems come from employees rather than from the managers themselves. Such expectations on the part of managers are unhealthy to both the organization and management.

While every management process involves risks, those associated with employee input can be reduced and potentially favorable results increased by following these guidelines:

Managers should clearly define the issues on which they are seeking employee input.

Managers should thoroughly explain these issues to the employees whose opinions are being solicited and the reasons for requesting their input.

An atmosphere of mutual trust must be established.

Feedback to employees at various stages of the process is essential.

Management must be prepared to act on employee input relatively promptly after it is given and in such a way that employees will perceive that their input was honestly considered.

The last guideline is perhaps the most critical one. Little else will destroy the effectiveness of employee input and severely damage the employer-employee relationship than employees' perceptions of a lack of sincerity on the part of management.

Employee input offers several advantages to the organization: The information is readily available, gathering it requires minimal expenditure of time and money, and most of the information received is reliable. Employee input can take many forms, including solicited and unsolicited, structured and unstructured, and group or individual. In the following sections, we will briefly examine examples of each.

Employee Surveys

While employee surveys can be as random as informally asking employees for their opinions, the most common approach is to solicit opinions in a more structured fashion in order to gain information, understand employees' perceptions more fully, and measure the level of employee acceptance or support of particular issues. Surveys can be beneficial in several ways, including, for example, learning more about employees' needs as they relate to the organization's benefit program or gaining insight into how employees perceive organizational policies and practices. Surveys can also help determine the level of employee support in unionization activity, say, or measure employees' acceptance of issues resulting from organizational transition.

Much of the activity associated with implementing surveys is a staff function, usually performed by human resources if it has the size and level of expertise needed. Otherwise, outside help can be sought. In any event, since managers are the primary link between employees and the organization, they not only should be familiar with the process of formulating and conducting employee surveys, but should have direct involvement, beginning with the decision of whether to utilize the survey tool through the final phases of evaluating the results and implementing action.

Like all forms of employee input, the main advantage of surveys is the relative ease with which the organization can gain a wide variety of information. The actual survey can be completed by employees with little interruption of production time. The two principal disadvantages are the difficulties frequently encountered in formulating a survey that fits the organization's needs and problems with heightened employee expectations as a result of the survey.

In deciding whether to use employee surveys, considerable effort should go into identifying the organization's needs to determine if a survey is appropriate. Whether a survey is developed by internal staff or by outside consultants, certain basic steps should be followed.

The objectives should be clearly stated and agreed on by the various levels of managers who will be making decisions and implementing the survey. Confusion and unrealistic expectations should be resolved beforehand. A plan of action should be formulated outlining who is responsible for each phase of the survey process. Management should attempt to anticipate employee reactions so they may be dealt with positively and supportively rather than defensively.

A decision should be made regarding the number of employees and the levels of the organization to be surveyed, with the objective of gaining the desired information most economically and expeditiously.

What methodology is best must be determined. Either interviews can be conducted with individual employees or questionnaires can be used, depending on the number of employees to be surveyed, availability of staff to conduct the survey, whether the survey questions are open ended, whether employee input is to be given anonymously, and similar factors.

How the survey will be implemented and how the results will be communicated to the employees should be carefully planned. All communications should be sincere and candid.

Obtaining the data is relatively easy; the major problem is how to assess it. Of course, the assumption is always that the survey questions have been well designed. Interpreting the information means comprehending not only what employees say but why they say it. Any action recommended can be suitable only if the data has been understood properly.

Decisions must be made as to what information or issues to act on and what others to either disregard or pursue at a later date. This step is crucial. A common pitfall is believing that every issue must be addressed. Whereas employees expect a relevant response, it is unlikely that they expect everything to be resolved.

Proposals as to how and when action is to be implemented should be based on the issues and how critical they are. Some actions may require further study by either management committees or employee task forces, while others can be adopted with little difficulty. Timing is also important. A delicate balance must be struck between allowing sufficient time to formulate action and being sure not to convey an image to employees of procrastination.

The survey results and proposed actions should be communicated to the employees with reasonable promptness. Again, candor and sincerity should guide management's communications with employees. This attitude is critical if management is to retain its credibility.

Sensing Groups

Employee "sensing" is a relatively new term given to a long-standing, familiar process. Stated simply, "sensing" is eliciting employee input. It is most commonly used to gather employees' perceptions or attitudes on various issues relating to the organization's personnel policies and practices. Like employee surveys, it can also be employed to solicit a wide variety of information and to measure the level of employee support of organizational issues and activities.

Outwardly, sensing appears to be less structured than conducting employee surveys. Actually, employee sensing is highly structured and requires careful planning and skilled execution. Normally, it is done in small group settings, but sensing sessions with individual employees are just as valuable.

Unlike employee surveys, sensing can be readily utilized by managers at any level. In fact, it is preferable that managers, as opposed to the human resources staff, be the ones who conduct sensing sessions, since the setting offers a unique opportunity to strengthen the employee-employer relationship beyond the daily routine. An exception should be made when the employees' concern or problem is their managers. In this situation, a better perspective can be brought by someone outside the organizational unit.

Human resources should assist in deciding what information to seek and in planning the methodology, teaching managers how to conduct the sessions, interpreting the results, and putting the action into effect. In situations requiring specialized handling, or in smaller organizations that do not have the depth of experience to conduct sensing sessions, carefully chosen outside consultants may be used.

A well-planned and well-executed sensing session can benefit the organization, the managers, and the employees. It provides the organization with a readily available source of information, much of which can be valuable in constructing or revamping employer-employee-relationship programs and practices. Sensing enhances management's image as interested in the employee as an individual with unique talent, ideas, and potential. Employees benefit from having a new outlet by which to share ideas with the organization. Perhaps the main potential disadvantage is that a poorly planned or improperly conducted session will lessen employees' confidence in the organization and particularly in their managers. Also, if sensing has failed, it becomes very difficult to introduce other employee input techniques.

When to use employee sensing depends in part on what type of information is being sought and how much interpretation will be required in evaluating it. Additionally, cost and expediency determine the feasibility of using sensing. The costs include both management and employee time spent in the sessions. All aspects of this tool are time consuming, and the process itself can be lengthy. However, unlike attitude surveys, which yield only raw information, sensing provides an opportunity to pursue, through personal contact, employees' lines of thinking, to observe their body language, and to listen to how they express themselves, all of which are powerful communicators and are observed directly.

The following guidelines are normally used in setting up employee sensing sessions. Since both employee surveys and employee sensing are input tools, certain steps are common to both; but distinct differences can be noted as well.

• In considering the use of employee sensing, the skill of managers or other persons who will conduct the session must be carefully assessed. This factor can be important in deciding whether to use managers or consultants.

• Thought must be given not only to what questions to ask but how to respond to controversial issues and issues that are off the subject. It takes special skills to allow employees to give their comments freely, while reasonably limiting the discussion to the planned topics.

• A free exchange of information is more likely to occur when employees are removed from their normal work environment. While off-site locations are helpful and may be cost-justified for sensing sessions involving managers or other higher-level employees who need an uninterrupted atmosphere, similar results can be achieved in a conference room within the organization but away from the employees' daily environment. The proper setting should free the employees from their daily routine and discourage interruptions.

• Whether to conduct sensing in groups or individually is influenced by how willing, on the basis of the strength of the employer-employee relationship, employees are to share information. The sensitivity of the issues to be discussed also helps determine whether the group or individual approach is chosen. In a group, the number of employees in a typical session should be small enough to allow for interaction of all members and large enough for group dynamics to encourage discussion. The number of employees can range from 6 to 14.

• Special care must be given to establishing rapport with employees at the beginning of each session. Unlike surveys, which rely on written communications to and from employees, sensing relies heavily on the spoken word. As indicated earlier, outwardly, sensing appears to be an informal process; but in reality it must be highly structured by planning what will be said, how, and when. An inappropriate comment or response from a manager could severely damage the session. Therefore, managers must be alert at all times.

• Solutions or commitments should never be given by managers during sensing sessions. Such off-the-cuff decisions could place the organization in an awkward position. Instead, employees should be assured that their input will be considered thoroughly.

• While the content of feedback given to employees is essential to any employee-input process, finding the appropriate methodology is just as crucial. The method chosen is particularly important to the success of future sensing sessions. Generally, feedback should be given in follow-up group sessions. The risk in giving employees the opportunity to question the decision made—or lack of action—by management is outweighed by the positive effects of the organization's demonstration of openness to its employees. Written feedback may sometimes be necessary because of time or cost factors, but it tends to be contrary to the purpose of the sensing tool.

Employee Task Forces

The purpose of an employee task force is to solicit input in a formal, structured manner on a particular issue. The value of this form of input is both in the ideas generated and in the acceptance of those ideas by employees outside the task force. Organizations that use task forces generally benefit from increased commitment and contribution of creativity by employees.

Task forces can have a variety of applications, including devising solutions to problems and recommending plans of action. In fact, they can be used whenever employee input is desirable and by managers at all levels without special training. Human resources should make the techniques that are needed available to managers and provide the appropriate support, including advice on how to conduct sessions and ways of implementing recommended action.

While outside consultants may be used to conduct employee task forces, in situations calling for specialized skills, such as in formulating a job-evaluation program, it is to the benefit of managers and the organization to have managers conduct the process in most cases. It provides managers with a new perspective on their employees and expands employees' image of management.

The advantages of using employee task forces include those that result from the "ownership" aspect of employees' feelings about their input. They are more apt to support organizational action that bears the imprint of their efforts. In addition, during the evaluation process employees experience some of the same frustrations routinely experienced by managers and therefore gain greater understanding of the management process and of their managers. The potential disadvantage relates to how well the process is conducted—management must exercise control but in a subtle fashion. Managers should consider the following suggestions in setting up and conducting task forces.

In general, management must have and must demonstrate considerable trust in its employees. The presence or absence of trust is reflected in the tone of the employer-employee relationship. If it is absent, employees will be quick to perceive it and as far as the task force is concerned will doubt its credibility. As a consequence, the results will be deficient. Management must also be prepared to utilize the input received from employees. If management has any reservations about its intention to do so, employee task forces should be avoided.

The task force must have credibility to the organization's employees. Therefore, selection of employees for it is critical. Depending on the proposed work of the task force, employees should generally be selected to reflect a cross-section of the organization. Such factors as age, sex, race, tenure with the organization, job level, and attitude strongly influence choice. Limiting the selection to only those employees who are outstanding performers or highly pro-organization defeats the objective of the process.

In explaining the purpose of the project to the task force members, its advisory capacity should be emphasized. It should be charged with recommending, as opposed to setting, policy or practice; and as potentially controversial issues arise during the process, this point should be reinforced. In addition, members should understand that the duration of the task force is contingent on the completion of its mission. No task force should be allowed to become permanent.

While some issues will typically be introduced that fall outside the objectives of the task force, discussion should, within reason, be limited to the mission at hand. Other issues should not be ignored, but their priority and the organization's capacity to deal with them must be considered.

On completion of the work of the task force, management must take special precautions to keep the members posted on its deliberations and what its decisions on the task force's recommendations are. When decisions are made, the task force members should be the first to be advised.

When the work of the task force involves action that will affect the organization's employees, the task force can be used to help announce or explain the end result to employees. Dealing on a peer basis increases the likelihood that employees will accept the results.

Quality-Control Circles

Unlike employee sensing groups and employee task forces, quality-control circles are designed to be relatively permanent. Of these three types of employee-input groups, quality-control circles come closest to being considered a structured form of participative management, whereby employee input can exceed the level of simple recommendations and deal with limited degrees of policy making.

Generally, quality-control circles are effective in increasing levels of production and decreasing production costs, although they are also used to resolve work-related problems. They have had considerable success in Japan but have met with only limited acceptance in the United States, mostly because of the strong hesitation among American managers to share authority with employees.

Unless the special expertise needed to implement quality-control circles is available in human resources, outside consultants who specialized in this particular employee input tool should be used. Some of these experts may have gained their experience in organizations that fostered the use of the quality-control-circle concept.

With each of these three employee input tools, the managers' role becomes more visible and critical than with other input systems. Conversely, human resources' role becomes less central and more one of staff support. The success of the quality-control process in particular depends on the role played by managers. There is little that human resources or any other staff function can do to facilitate its success without support from management at all levels.

The advantages of quality-control groups are that production levels usually increase, sometimes significantly, and work-related problems such as absenteeism, lateness, and poor work quality typically decrease. Additionally, in becoming more understanding of managers' problems, employees are apt to become more supportive as well. Many of managers' gate-keeping problems, such as attempting to improve employee attendance, are often solved by employee involvement in quality-control circles. Thus managers are free to focus on other needs of the organizational unit. Finally, successful results of quality-control circles often increase employees' desire to become involved in other activities of the organization and to find new avenues for their input. The disadvantages are for the most part a matter of the organization's perceptions based on its value system.

Of the three input tools discussed thus far, the quality-control circle requires the most deliberation before it can be implemented. The more deeply rooted an organization is in an authoritarian management style, the less likely it is that this tool will be accepted by its managers. At best, even in employee-oriented environments, managers may not be able to commit themselves sufficiently to the concept for one reason or another, typically because managers feel they must be the creators of new ideas and the problem solvers. To allow employees a share in creativity or problem solving is often perceived as a managerial weakness. In essence, adopting a quality-control circle requires a change in management's thinking, particularly at the executive level, and a change in the organization's value system. Successful results require commitment, time, and effort. Assuming that management has thoroughly considered the feasibility of implementing the quality-control-circle concept and is committed to it, the following guidelines generally apply:

• Training and development of the managers who will be involved must be the first activity. Gaining their support and commitment at this stage is critical. The fact that the process can in the long run lessen managers' burdens should be emphasized. Aside from receiving training, managers will frequently need encouragement in developing new attitudes toward employee involvement. This process requires reinforcement from executive-level management.

• Extensive communication with employees should begin well in advance of the planned implementation date. As with most new ideas, employees will experience varying levels of anxiety and reluctance and have doubts about management's intentions. If an organization is unionized, the union should be made a partner to the process. The objective is to win employees' support or at the very least their willingness to try the idea.

• Unlike employee task forces, where the objective is to select a representative group of employees, the selection of employees to participate in quality-control circles is predetermined or otherwise limited by the objective of the quality-control circle in relation to the jobs and work processes. The strength of the tool depends on developing a highly cohesive group of employees within the organizational unit.

• Once the quality-control circle is in place, immediate results should not be expected. The process has to mature through a cycle natural to group behavior. The group must first learn to work together. This phase involves dealing with individual controversy within the group, coping with frustration, and establishing direction as a group. During this period, managers should avoid providing the solutions to problems. To do so would encourage too much reliance on the managers, thereby negating the group's value.

• Encouragement and feedback on the circle's progress must be freely given both to managers and, from the managers, to employees.

• Compromise between managers and employees will emerge as a major factor in accepting and implementing group decisions. This new arrangement will be difficult for some managers accustomed to an authoritarian style. However, managers may see the validity of compromise if they understand that although differences of opinion may exist between managers and employees on how to implement the idea, the end result or benefit of an idea is usually the same.

• The mission given to the quality-control circle should be substantial enough to be challenging, but should also be limited so as not to be unachievable. It is also recommended that the group be allowed to experience success and gather confidence before its mission is broadened. Well-seasoned groups have proved to be a tremendous source of help in increasing productivity, resolving production problems, and reducing costs.

Unsolicited Individual Employee-Input Systems

Individual employee-input systems allow employees to give their input to management at their own discretion, rather than relying on management to solicit it. The most common device used is the suggestion system, whereby employees are encouraged to share their ideas related to work improvement with the organization, usually in return for some form of compensation award or other kind of recognition. We touched briefly on "pipeline" programs as a valuable form of upward communication in Chapter 6. Here, we will view the suggestion program in the context of its value as employee input.

In general, a well-rounded input system should always allow for several forms of unsolicited employee input, including opinions, comments, and questions on the organization's operations, policies, and practices. The value of having an unsolicited input system that encourages many forms of input includes not only having access to employees' ideas but through their questions and opinions being able to ascertain the level of employee understanding and degree of support on various issues. Some systems allow for employee complaints of a general nature, not to be confused with a concern-handling procedure.

Managers benefit from an increased awareness of employee-related issues and, to the extent that they participate in responding to employee input, are perceived as being concerned with their employees. Managers should be directly involved in designing and implementing this kind of employee-input system as well as in administering and promoting it.

In considering the feasibility of such an individual employee-input system, a number of factors should be kept in mind. The organization, particularly through its first-level managers, must be receptive to employees' input and willing to use their suggestions, evaluate their opinions, and resolve their complaints. A positive attitude toward employee input is the key to the success of any input system of this kind. The system must, in fact, encourage input. For the employee, the incentive to offer suggestions, usually in the form of some monetary award, must be worthwhile. The organization must also demonstrate that it sincerely wants employees' opinions, which can be measured by how thoroughly it considers them and what it eventually does with them. In addition, employees must not be penalized, either directly or covertly, for voicing complaints.

Forms should be uncomplicated, easy to use, and readily available to employees without their having to ask for them. Generally, good locations for forms are in the vicinity of employee bulletin boards, time clocks, entrances, and lunchroom facilities.

Conscientious administration of the system is important. All employee input must be promptly acted on, and if delays are necessary, employees should be so advised. While routine administration of the system is typically performed by the human resources staff, managers should be involved in evaluating and responding to employees' suggestions, questions, opinions, and complaints as they pertain to their particular organizational units. Usually, a committee is formed to evaluate the suggestions. While some organizations involve employees in these committees, employees should not participate if the system deals with employee complaints and opinions as well as suggestions and questions.

It is important that it be the suggestion, opinion, or complaint that is evaluated, not the employee. The evaluation of good ideas should not be clouded by a manager's prejudices toward a particular employee. Objectivity is important. The criteria for evaluating suggestions should be clearly established and communicated to employees, as should the procedures for handling employees' opinions, questions, and complaints. Including this information in employee handbooks is one such method of communication.

Awards and other forms of recognition must be presented to the employee in such a manner as to demonstrate the organization's appreciation of the input. Whatever the award or commendation, it is important to be aware of the value of peer recognition.

If the system is to be ongoing, it must be continuously promoted. Employee suggestions and ideas that are used by the organization should be publicized in the house organ. Generally, employees should be recognized by managers individually for their input, even if their suggestions are not accepted. The objective is to encourage employee input, and recognition is a proven motivator.

By means of reports and other mechanisms, managers should be kept informed by human resources of employee input that is relevant to their organizational units and to the total organization.

They should be given training periodically by human resources on how to encourage, handle, and acknowledge employee input.

One of the side benefits of an individual unsolicited employee-input system is that it helps to identify the more creative thinkers in the organization for possible further career development through training for higher-level jobs.

Employee-Communications Tools and Techniques

Despite the availability of a wide variety of materials and techniques ranging from basic-training films to manuals on conducting sensitivity-group sessions, many organizations suffer from inadequate communications with their employees and sometimes with their managers as well. In fact, most employee-relations problems can be traced to ineffective communications.

Much has been written on both communication and communications tools in recent years. Interest in the subject of organization communication techniques has traditionally been high. It has become apparent that if the desire to communicate openly is absent or at a low level, the use of training or other techniques to improve communications will have little effect. Effective communication occurs only when people truly want to communicate. To illustrate this point, consider two people from different cultures, each of whom speaks a different language. They are brought together by a common purpose, say the convention of a professional or fraternal organization. Despite the barriers, they find ways to communicate, often with considerable effectiveness, because each has the desire to do so.

Why is it, then, that in organizations made up of members speaking the same language and coming from the same culture, people cannot communicate as effectively as the two strangers? And if the desire is not present, how can it be instilled? Solutions to this last question may be easy to identify but are often difficult to effect. The communication patterns of organizations are deeply rooted in their organizational cultures, value systems, past practices, and other factors that result from, and are continually reinforced by, various attitudes. The principal one, for purposes of this discussion, is the organization's attitude toward its employees and sometimes toward its managers.

Some organizations' attitudes toward employees may be in need of improvement but are so deeply ingrained that even executive-level management faces enormous difficulty in trying to change them. Regardless, managers should not become discouraged from looking for ways to improve communications with their employees. At best, it is a continual process calling for commitment from all levels of management.

On a more positive note, it should be emphasized that managers can significantly influence communications within their own organizational units. As a starting point, they should focus on understanding how good communications can benefit them, their employees, and the organization, and why it is important. Effective communication—and the attitude it represents—forms the basis for cooperation. A high level of cooperation is required for high productivity and profitability in an organization. The essence of the manager's role is to help the organization achieve these goals. How successful managers are in doing so is determined by the level of cooperation between them and their employees, which is in turn determined by how healthy communications are between them.

To improve communications in their particular units, managers, besides participating in various training and development programs, can readily use the following basic tools and techniques at little cost beyond the investment of time and effort. Managers should:

• Be sensitive to employees as individuals by recognizing the talents and creativity of each. If managers do not become aware of this talent, how can the organization benefit from it? Discovering employees' abilities requires that managers reevaluate their attitudes toward each employee. Attitudes strongly influence how people communicate and deal with each other.

• Sharpen listening skills. Until recently, the emphasis had been on developing public-speaking skills to the detriment of listening skills. Managers should learn to listen, not only to what is said but how it is said and, equally important, what is not said. Frequently, some of employees' most important messages—their real feelings—are actually communicated by their silence or reticence on various subjects.

• Attempt to understand the why behind what employees say. Learning to identify employees' reasons for certain comments helps managers understand the meaning often obscured by the words.

• Be open with employees. Not only should managers be accessible to their employees, but they should be perceived as being interested in and wanting to understand them. This atmosphere is achieved in part by nurturing mutual trust and confidence.

• Just as managers need recognition, affirmation, and feedback, so do their subordinates. Managers should recognize this and give feedback freely.

Beyond these fairly simple techniques, a wealth of material is available on the subject. Because the principle is so important, it bears reemphasizing—good communications depend on attitude. Managers, by virtue of their role, must assume the lead in fostering better employee-employer communications.

Managers have a vested interest not only in the level of communication in their organizational unit, but in that of the total organization. If managers can help shape this overall communication process, they should not hesitate to do so. Since traditionally, organizations have fewer opportunities to communicate with employees than employees have to communicate among themselves, organizations need to be coordinated and precise in their downward communications. In addition, they must maximize those relatively few opportunities to communicate formally with employees by making a conscientious and well-planned effort.

Generally, most of an organization's formal communication with its employees is coordinated by human resources, which uses various standard tools, depending mostly on the size of the organization and its available resources. Managers should be familiar with these tools and, while they may not have direct control over them, should provide input into their usage.

Employee Bulletin Boards

Bulletin boards provide employees with a readily acceptable means of receiving timely information about the organization and their particular organizational unit. Typical information displayed on bulletin boards ranges from postings required by EEO, OSHA, Fair Labor Standards Act, and similar laws to notices about available in-house jobs and announcements of special events.

The value of bulletin boards is that they convey information quickly and with relative ease. They are not intended to compete with or duplicate house organs, which by virtue of their lengthy preparation requirements are used principally to furnish information that does not have a critical time factor. Unfortunately, the usefulness of bulletin boards is frequently diminished by indiscriminate and untimely posting of information.

While human resources is usually in charge of posting and removing information, managers should not hesitate to use bulletin boards to supplement their communications with employees. In deciding whether the posting of a particular piece of information is appropriate and will be effective, managers should consider how soon employees need the information, whether immediate employee feedback is desired, and whether meeting individually with employees or holding employee meetings would be better.

Regardless of who takes care of posting information, organizations should have a nonsolicitation policy, which not only protects the organization from inadvertently distributing information from outside entities during company time but restricts posting to items related to the organization and approved by management.

Employee House Organs

The objective of employee house organs, whether limited in scope, such as newsletters, or more comprehensive, such as employee magazines, is to assimilate employees into the organization through sharing of information. Whether it succeeds depends on its acceptance by employees—how many read it and understand its message and how their view of the organization is shaped by it.

The publication of a house organ is staff oriented and is typically assigned to human resources. The house organ is, however, a reflection of the total organization and therefore requires its active support, particularly that of its managers. Frequently, managers overlook the value of house organs in the managerial role and fail to capitalize on the opportunity to voice their views on what its general content should be and to supply material.

One of the main difficulties in sustaining a successful house organ is finding ongoing sources of information of the kind that will help it fulfill its objectives. Usually the content is of four types:

1. Information about the organization, its future plans, benefits and policies, new services or products, and personnel changes as well as financial data.
2. Interpretation of news and current events in terms of their impact on the future of the organization and its employees.
3. Management's views on controversial issues.
4. Entertainment that is geared toward discussing employees and their accomplishments, both on and off the job, presented with a certain amount of humor and human interest.

Managers are in an excellent position to know their employees and what their accomplishments are. By sharing information and insights on their employees' interests with the human resources staff, managers can help widen readership of the house organ while giving recognition and affirmation to particular employees.

Employee Handbooks

Since managers are responsible for setting the tone of the day-to-day employee-employer relationship and in large part determine whether it is successful, assistance in the form of a well-developed employee handbook can be extremely helpful to them in their task. Thus, while the handbook is essential to the organization as a whole, it is particularly important as an aid to management. Since they have a vested interest, managers should not hesitate to offer input on what is to appear in the handbook and even how certain topics should be expressed. Although human resources usually constructs the employee handbook, material should never be finalized without review and approval by managers, who will be the ones eventually called on to explain the contents to employees and enforce as required.

Recognizing that the handbook is often a new employee's first exposure to the organization's policies and practices after the orientation program, the material should be readable and easy to understand and the tone should be cordial, since it reflects the organization's employee-relations philosophy. A poorly designed and badly written handbook is more a liability than an asset to an organization. The following are the usual categories of information contained in employee handbooks:

- The organization's history, the products or services rendered, and the organizational structure.
- Payroll procedures and employment practices, including hiring policies.
- Compensation and benefits offered, ranging from earning merit increases to benefits coverage and eligibility.
- Opportunities through job posting, availability of training, promotion procedures, and other topics dealing with employee growth and development.

- Employee services available, including lunchroom and parking facilities, health services, employee activities associations, and credit unions.
- Employee responsibilities, disciplinary policies and procedures, and concern handling.

Whenever it is feasible, managers should participate in explaining the handbook to their employees and should distribute handbook revisions to them. The more managers are involved as communicators, the greater the assurance that the handbook will be used successfully.

Meetings with Employees

Meetings between managers and employees provide an excellent opportunity for managers to improve two-way communications and to enhance their image to employees as being people oriented. Managers can learn to use this technique successfully with minimal training from human resources.

Employee meetings are designed to encourage a reasonably free flow of information between managers and employees. They are used when organizations desire not only to inform their employees on a certain issue, but to allow for employees' questions and comments. To this extent, meetings have a distinct advantage over house organs, bulletin boards, and similar techniques that do not permit immediate questions or feedback. They work best when mutual trust and confidence exist between employees and management and can be successfully used to help shape employees' opinions. Before instituting employee meetings, consider these points:

- The purpose of the meetings should be clearly understood by the managers involved and their employees.
- Meetings should be properly prepared. Poorly planned meetings will defeat their purpose.
- The number of participants in any one meeting should be large enough to encourage group discussion and small enough to

avoid having to deny any employees the opportunity to ask questions and engage in discussion.

• The role of managers in meetings as purveyors of information and coordinators of discussion is crucial. The job of discussion leader requires more skill because the tone of the meeting must assure employees that they do not risk reprisals or loss of face with their comments or questions.

• Using the techniques previously discussed to enhance their communications skills, particularly those dealing with effective listening, managers should attempt to discern employee sentiments on issues being discussed at meetings.

• Any success from employee meetings will be lost unless improved communications are sustained by the ongoing, day-to-day dealings between managers and employees.

Employee-Assistance Tools and Techniques

In part because organizations are recognizing more and more their substantial investment in employees and in part because employees are demanding more supportive services from their employers, many organizations are evaluating various employee-assistance programs and practices. Previously, most organizations offered only those forms of assistance dealing solely with work-related issues.

The objective of employee-assistance tools, some of which will be discussed in this section, is to preserve employees as productive members of the organization. Frequently, managers mistakenly believe that such tools are designed just to keep employees happy with their relationship with the organization. Their accent instead should be on maintaining the high level of morale that is necessary for productivity. High morale is best encouraged when employees feel that the organization is interested in their well-being and will help them if they are in need.

It is self-evident that an organization's interest in its employees cannot be purely altruistic. Organizations need not and should not compete with outside social welfare sources in helping employees. This role is not organizations' primary responsibility and tends to confuse the employer-employee relationship. Organizations should help employees only when it benefits the work relationship.

Employee-Assistance Programs

The history of employee-assistance programs provides an excellent example of what the objectives and the limits of an organization's involvement in helping its employees should be. Such programs were originally developed to deal principally with alcoholism. As society's understanding of serious personal problems grew, these kinds of programs came to embrace a wider range of situations. Today, many employee-assistance programs cover drug abuse, emotional illness, marital difficulties, and other family crises, in addition to alcoholism.

While essentially these are problems of a personal nature, it is unrealistic to expect employees to be able to leave them at home. So, to the extent that personal problems affect employees' daily behavior and performance on the job, they become management's problems. Managers are therefore forced, however reluctantly, to identify and assist troubled employees.

It is because of the growing understanding of the intent and the potential benefits of employee-assistance programs that more organizations are adopting them. While human resources usually sets up the program and sees to its day-to-day administration, managers really determine its success because of their unique position to observe and gauge employees' productivity and behavior.

Early identification by managers of job-performance problems or changes in employees' behavior is critical. Equally important is prompt action by managers. Working within the framework of the employee-assistance program, problems adversely affecting employees may be quickly resolved or, at the very least, given immediate attention, thus averting a more serious or more costly problem for the organization. These guidelines should be followed in a typical employee-assistance program:

• The program must have the full commitment of executive management. In essence, it is a highly visible reflection of the value an organization places on its employees.

• All levels of management must be charged with identifying problems and taking action promptly in accordance with the program's philosophy and procedures. Problem identification cannot be limited to a staff function such as human resources.

• It is not the intent of employee-assistance programs to place managers in the role of professional counselors, or diagnosticians, only that they be trained in problem identification and in the referral of employees to sources of help.

• Training of managers in the use of the program is a continuous process. In addition, constant reinforcement is necessary to ensure its ongoing success.

• The organization's benefits package should be supportive of the program. For example, the health and major medical insurance coverage should include employee counseling and treatment of alcoholism and emotional illness. Medical leave of absence and other mechanisms to allow employees time off for treatment should be coordinated with the program.

• Close working relationships between managers and human resources should be cultivated. After identifying work-related problems, managers should confer with human resources to determine whether outside professional help is needed, how to refer the employee, and similar questions.

• In any arrangement for treatment of an employee by outside professionals, human resources should keep managers advised as to the various steps involved, the employee's progress, any temporary adjustments necessitated in the employee's job, and similar factors. All matters pertaining to the employee's problem and treatment should be handled by human resources and managers with utmost confidentiality.

• Employees should be assured that their future in the organization will not be jeopardized and that they will not be otherwise penalized by seeking help through the program. Decisions affecting employees' futures should be made on the basis of job performance, not whether they have experienced some personal problem and sought treatment.

• Whether professional help is offered within the organization or by outside sources is mostly a function of the organization's size and resources. Small organizations usually cannot justify the expense of maintaining counselors, psychologists, or other professionals on their staffs. Generally, professional help should be given by outside sources primarily because of the value from employees' perception that objectivity and confidentiality have been exercised in the handling of their problems.

In evaluating whether to implement an employee-assistance program, organizations would do well to recognize that there are few if any feasible alternatives. In today's complex society, the incidence of personal problems will inevitably increase and will be more frequent in the workplace. Employee-assistance programs provide a feasible way to deal with such situations.

Career Counseling

Since organizations are made up of people, the growth of an organization depends on the growth of its people. Increased job knowledge, development of skills, and broader application of abilities by employees come about in part through job experience, training and development, and exposure to opportunities within the organization. Before growth can take place, however, employees must have the desire. And although the desire to grow is the first step, there must also be external stimuli. A large part of the manager's job is to provide such stimuli. The occasions for managers to do so are many and varied. Recognition for a job well done, acknowledgement of individual talent, and praise or affirmation are but a few of the ways in which managers can encourage employees to grow professionally.

Another particularly important way is through career counseling, which is a tool that managers, while responding to the needs within the organization for expansion of its human resources, can also use in helping to develop the career of a particular employee.

The perception of career counseling as a highly complex process accounts for why many managers are skeptical as to its merits. Some managers also withhold their support of career counseling because it increases the possibility of losing valuable employees to other units of the organization. Such a view is shortsighted, however. If employees do not see opportunities for growth, they are likely to leave the organization altogether. In its simplest form, successful career counseling should embrace the following concepts:

• To be most effective career counseling should take place within the context of the needs of the total organization. Accordingly, employees' growth and development should not be limited to their immediate organizational units.

• Preferably, career counseling should be part of a more comprehensive plan designed by the organization for maximum use of its employees. Typically, such plans are part of the organization's long-range human resources or staffing programs.

• Organizations must fully support the objectives of career counseling—namely, employee growth and development—by providing the necessary support mechanisms. Typically this support involves offering training and development to employees through in-house or outside programs, much of which was discussed in Chapter 5.

• Managers should rely on human resources for training in career-counseling techniques and for whatever other forms of support it has to offer, including follow-up counseling for employees by human resources staff members and testing as deemed feasible.

• If no formalized career-counseling programs are offered by the organization, managers can still encourage employee development by making use of the many situations that lend themselves to counseling opportunities, ranging from employee-performance interviews to the routine, day-to-day contact with employees.

Because of the need to remain competitive and to guard against an eventually obsolete work force, organizations have little choice other than to develop some approach to career counseling. Regardless of how informal the approach, it is better than none at all.

Preretirement Counseling

Preretirement counseling provides employees with information and assistance to help them plan for retirement and ease their transition from the workplace into a new environment. Until recently, most organizations lacked even the rudiments of a formalized approach to severing their working relationship with retiring employees. Even today, all too many organizations narrowly confine their view of responsibility toward retiring employees to awarding the proverbial gold watch.

How organizations treat long-term employees nearing retirement age reflects the state of the employer-employee relationship and will be scrutinized increasingly by younger employees. So providing services to retiring employees can also have an indirect benefit, namely, a positive influence on how remaining employees view the organization. A preretirement program, generally administered by human resources, should offer to its staff members:

- Financial planning, which includes help in preparing for financial needs, advice on how to handle a surviving spouse's estate, reviewing wills, and evaluating insurance needs.
- Health planning, which focuses on advising employees on health care, both physical and mental, and on handling health limitations brought about by age.
- Activity planning, which deals with discussion of life-styles accompanying retirement and maintaining purpose in life through meaningful activity.

The program should be open to employees about three to five years in advance of their projected retirement dates and should focus on helping retirees make the appropriate attitudinal adjustment as well as adapt to the change in life-style. Since most preretirement programs are voluntary, as any program of this type should be, they need management's active support.

Employee-Relations Tools and Techniques

While all of the previously discussed tools and techniques affect the organization's relationship with its employees and can therefore be generally classified as employee-relations tools, some techniques are specifically designed to be applied to the organization's employer-employee relations.

These tools, perhaps more than those previously discussed, require total commitment from everyone in the organization. Maintaining productive employee relations cannot be assigned to any specialty function; rather it is a basic responsibility of every manager as well as of human resources and other supporting staffs.

The following are some of the more basic employee-relations tools and techniques. They serve as examples to illustrate, in summary form, many of the principles discussed throughout this chapter to foster positive and productive employee relations.

Programs to Resolve Employee Concerns and Problems

Whenever people work together, problems inevitably arise. How they are dealt with and resolved has a marked influence on future working relationships in an organization. Concerns and problems that remain unsettled usually lead to any number of undesirable results. The objective of programs that address employee difficulties is to provide a readily accessible, formal mechanism through which employees can obtain prompt, consistent, and definitive action by management without fear of reprisal.

However, such programs are intended to supplement, not substitute for, the availability of managers to their employees that is an essential part of the ongoing work relationship.

Use of the term "grievance handling" to describe such programs actually works against their objectives. The programs' philosophy, particularly as reinforced through day-to-day work relationships, should encourage discussion of employees' concerns with management before they reach the crisis level. The emphasis should be on resolving work-related difficulties as quickly as possible, as opposed to taking a reactive approach and listening to employees only after a situation has developed into a genuine grievance.

The role of human resources in a program to resolve employee concerns, unlike its role in many of the previously discussed tools, is very limited. Aside from the initial design and implementation of the program, its only involvement is usually in counseling managers on how to approach the issues brought up by employees. Managers, on the other hand, have the critical role. Their success is measured by how well they demonstrate their capacity to:

Respect employees and treat them in a dignified manner.

Facilitate an environment where employees want to discuss work-related concerns or problems openly.

Be alert to sources of employee irritations.

Take prompt and effective action whenever possible to eliminate or reduce the causes of irritation.

Be perceived as a person of high integrity who deals fairly with employees.

Be perceived as a manager who will stand up for employees or back them up when necessary.

Be approachable.

Have a genuine interest in employees' welfare and development.

Forms for use by employees in forwarding their concerns or

problems to management should be conveniently available. Employees should not have to request them from their managers. Resolution of a problem should begin with the employee's immediate manager, unless the manager is part of the problem. Review of employee's concerns by higher-level management should be allowed in the event employees either are dissatisfied with the response given by their immediate manager or desire to have it reviewed by higher management.

Time limitations for a response from managers should be built into the process to ensure that employees' concerns are addressed promptly. Whereas such programs by their very nature have an air of formality about them, solutions to problems should be attempted in an informal environment created by managers. For example, even though managers may respond in writing, they should meet with the employee and deliver the written response by hand, at the same time giving an explanation.

The program should continually be publicized to employees to encourage its use, with the accent on management's desire to resolve employee's concerns quickly in the incipient stage. Accordingly, the program should be outlined in employee handbooks, promoted in the organization's house organ, and in general, be given as much exposure as possible.

Recognition Programs

Recognition programs are designed to formally and publicly give affirmation to employees for their contributions and to encourage the continuation of their good performance and involvement. Such programs are not limited to employees' contributions within the organization but may encompass recognition for civic involvement. The use and scope of recognition programs are only as limited as the organization's creativity and desire. The following are examples of some of the more typical programs:

• Attendance recognition. The objective is to provide an appropriate form of award or affirmation that will be seen as worthwhile by employees and thus will serve to foster good attendance and reduce lateness. The success of the program lies in the value employees place on the form of recognition received. A potential disadvantage of this program to organizations using a merit system of employee-performance assessment to determine salary increases is that in essence a key performance factor, attendance, has been removed from the performance assessment and rewarded separately.

• Support of community involvement. Some organizations, because of their high profile in the community, encourage employees to become involved in civic activities. Aside from encouraging and acknowledging this kind of involvement through service awards and publicity in the organization's house organ, organizations sometimes provide additional support to involved employees by allowing time off from work or making available such services as word processing or printing.

• Performance recognition. To stimulate creativity and productivity, some organizations offer awards and other forms of recognition to employees who make significant contributions to the success of the organization. What is recognized as a unique performance contribution is as varied as the organization. Such contributions can include articles published in trade journals, inventions or patents, technical contributions, and improved work processes.

• Service recognition. The purpose of such awards is to recognize employees, in essence, for their seniority. While many organizations have service recognition programs, their value is questionable. Long-term employee service can be either a blessing or a curse depending on the performance of the employee. Additionally, some traditional awards with only symbolic value have little meaning to younger generations. Since the worth of such programs is limited, the cost to the organization should be kept low.

• Safety awards. In industrial environments or other work situations where potentially greater health hazards exist than in offices, safety awards have the distinct value of focusing employee attention on the need to comply with safety procedures. Typically regarded as a lackluster topic, employees' awareness of work safety requires constant promotion and large doses of creativity.

Job-Posting Programs

Organizations frequently overlook the unused talent within their own ranks. By confining its selection of candidates for available jobs to outside applicants, the organization deprives itself of this valuable resource. The purpose of a job-posting program is to increase the number of qualified applicants for jobs and to provide an additional means for employees to grow with the organization. A well-constructed job-posting program can benefit both the organization and its employees.

Managers can be instrumental in the success of the program by openly encouraging their subordinates to bid on jobs in other organizational units and by being receptive to applicants from outside their organizational unit for higher-level jobs. Some managers are reluctant to lose good employees. Conversely, they frequently use higher-level job openings within their unit to reward their own employees rather than opening such opportunities to the rest of the organization. This practice does not always ensure that the most qualified applicant gets the job. Recommended guidelines for job-posting programs include:

- To establish the credibility of the program, reduce the likelihood of favoritism, and ensure that the most qualified applicants will be considered, all jobs should be posted, including management jobs.
- If organizations are uncomfortable about posting all positions at all levels and prefer to limit posting to jobs within certain levels or salary grades, at the very least all jobs within those designated levels or ranges should be posted without exception.
- The job-posting notice should provide employees with the

appropriate information about the position, including job title, salary range, summary of job duties, required education, skills, and experience, and whom to contact and by when.
* Notices should be posted in locations convenient to employees and should remain posted for a reasonable time period to ensure that employees have an opportunity to become aware of the job.
* Unsuccessful bidders should be promptly notified, and whenever possible, career counseling should be made available to them.

Human resources coordinates the program. Generally, it is responsible for posting the notices, initially screening the applicants, arranging interviews with managers, monitoring for compliance with employment laws and practices, processing the related paperwork, and similar tasks. Managers, just as in the hiring process discussed in Chapter 2, should make the selection decision.

Employee Organizations
Depending on the size of the organization and the availability of support mechanisms, principally through human resources, employee organizations can reinforce good employee relations. The objective of most employee organizations is twofold: to expand employee services and to increase opportunities for involvement in the organization.

In developing an employee organization, its purpose must be clearly formulated and agreed on, mainly by management but also by the employees involved. The greatest risk is that an employee organization can become a sounding board for unrelated employee issues. To avoid this situation, management should form a close liaison with the employee organization and provide guidance to assure that the group is not diverted from its original intent. Some of the more common kinds of organizations allowing for employee involvement include the following:

Activities associations. The basic purpose of this kind of association is to promote fellowship and goodwill through leisure-time activities and certain work-related activities. Membership is typically voluntary; dues are required and are frequently matched by contributions from the organization. A constitution and bylaws govern the association, and it is administered by a board of trustees elected by the members. Separate committees are designated to plan activities.

Participation in activities is frequently not limited to employees but is open to employees' families as well. Typical activities include team sports, annual picnics, and excursions.

Community service funds. In response to the need to support charitable civic organizations and other worthwhile causes, organizations have encouraged the formation of community service funds by its employees. Contributions are usually made through payroll deductions to a group fund that then disperses the donations, rather than have employees make individual contributions to various causes.

Generally, community service fund organizations involve voluntary participation, are governed by a board of trustees elected by its members, and have a constitution and bylaws.

Credit unions. One of the more popular kinds of employee organizations, credit unions provide a convenient method for employees to save money and obtain low-cost loans. While credit unions should be administered by employees, with minimal involvement from the organization, management should be assured that the operation of the credit union is in compliance with applicable federal and state laws and regulations.

Retired employees organizations. All too frequently organizations write off their retirees, who have often provided many years of service to the organization and contributed to its growth and success. In coordination with preretirement programs, discussed previously, retired employee groups can benefit organizations beyond the value of goodwill, through participation in orientation programs for new employees, counseling employees who are planning to retire, and representing the organization in civic activities.

Service award organizations. Perhaps the most typical service award organization is the Quarter Century Club for employees with 25 years of service. Such clubs provide recognition to employees and demonstrate the organization's regard for long service. For the benefits derived, they cost organizations relatively little money and time.

Since much of the work of developing and coordinating activities for employee organizations is staff oriented, the various responsibilities should be assigned to the human resources function. Managers should not hesitate, however, to offer input concerning what organizations should be formed and the role of each in the parent organization.

Tools and Techniques to Develop Relationships with External Organizations

Increasingly, organizations are using their managers to interface with other organizations in activities ranging from community involvement to joint ventures with educational institutions. Previously, the external affairs role in organizations was usually performed by specialty functions, such as public relations, community affairs, and to a lesser extent, human resources. Among the benefits of involving managers in external affairs activities are the following:

• Managers, in being called on to represent the organization, have to learn more about it and in doing so usually develop an expanded perception of both the organization and their individual role in it.

• This expanded perception helps managers understand the importance of their internal role and that of their organizational unit in terms of the organization's mission.

• In learning more about the organization as a whole, managers tend to become more understanding and supportive of roles and functions other than their own.

• An organization's credibility and standing in the community are usually enhanced when people have an opportunity to learn about the organization from someone directly involved in its management.

• Using management in this role alleviates the need to hire additional staff to perform certain of these specialized functions.

Additionally, participation in external affairs allows managers more direct control of the results of certain activities in which they have a vested interest. As these activities pertain to the topics discussed in this chapter, the following are offered:

Internships and Work-Study Programs

Generally, human resources is responsible for cultivating relationships with educational institutions and otherwise developing sources of potential employees. It performs this task, in part, by setting up internships and similar work-study programs whereby students gain practical experience in their field through special assignments in the organization. The organization, in turn, has the opportunity to evaluate the student-worker as a possible candidate for future employment. At the very least, the organization benefits from the public relations value of the internship among the student-worker's peers. This favorable impression can help the organization's recruiting from that institution by enhancing its image.

Managers have a vested interest in the success of internships and work-study programs because they and their organizational units benefit from additional sources of potential personnel. In addition they can offer valuable assistance to human resources in structuring the work assignments for the internship and in receiving interns into their organizational unit. Because managers are viewed as the experts in their particular operation, they have a distinct advantage to both their organization and the educational institution, not possessed by human resources. Through the expertise managers share with them, both students and faculty are exposed to knowledge and, particularly, practical experience they might not otherwise encounter, especially at the student's level of development.

Managers should be encouraged to expand their involvement in internships by visiting educational institutions, discussing their operation with faculty and students, and otherwise coordinating the internship with human resources and the institution.

Cooperative Ventures with Outside Institutions

Beyond internships and work-study programs, a variety of additional ways are available by which managers can share their expertise with outside organizations for the mutual benefits previously outlined. By conducting guest lectures and seminars, managers can bring their specialized knowledge into the classroom. In addition, they can arrange for outside faculty to take part in programmed participation projects within the organization. In essence, managers should work with the human resources staff in finding ways to use their talents beyond the confines of their immediate job environments. In this capacity, they represent a vast resource for organizations that is often not fully utilized.

Computerized Employee-Information Systems

Computers have revolutionized the operation of organizations and will continue to do so. With their introduction in the late 1940s, they were initially looked on with mixed emotions. Some managers viewed them as luxuries to be afforded, often questionably, only by large, prosperous organizations. Furthermore, their value to organizations was largely unproved.

Today, computers can be found in even the smallest organizations. It is no longer a question of whether to use them, but rather how. Many young people now entering management have often received considerable training in the use of computers as part of their college education. It is a rare higher-level educational institution that does not offer students at least minimal exposure to computers and the field of electronic data processing. Managers who heretofore were ignorant about computers recognize their value and seek out sources of knowledge. The popularity of computers was brought about by many factors. Among them are:

- The large volume of information that any organization of any size is required to handle necessitated that more economically feasible alternatives be found to the traditional method of employing large clerical staffs.
- As the pace of organizational life increased, the need for quick retrieval of information became critical.
- Aside from storage and retrieval of information, computers quickly demonstrated their potential for assisting management in the decision-making process through a wide variety of applications.
- Computers, principally as a result of their use in America's aerospace projects beginning in the late 1950s, are relied on as a valuable tool in problem solving.

As technology improved, the use of computers increased. No longer are all computers highly sophisticated pieces of equipment, costing vast sums of money to purchase or rent and requiring a highly technical staff to operate. Technology has placed the computer within the financial reach of nearly every organization. With the advent of mini- and micro-computers, many are even used in the home. As much as computers are being utilized today, some forecasters predict that this is just the beginning. Clearly, computers are here to stay, and it is the wise manager who learns to benefit from this valuable management tool.

Understandably, computers can be employed in a wide variety of ways. In fact, their use is only as limited as management's creativity. It is not surprising, therefore, that they have been embraced by the human resources function. With the increased need to store and retrieve employee-related information brought about largely by such federal laws and regulations as equal employment opportunity, affirmative action, and occupational safety and health, and the wider scope of employee benefit plans, human resources functions were attracted to the convenience and economies offered by computers. Through the availability of low-cost mini-computers, of software packages especially designed for human resources applications, and of time-sharing plans offered by electronic data processing service organizations, even the smallest human resources operation can afford this tool.

While many of the direct applications of a human-resources-based computer system are understandably geared toward assisting human resources in fulfilling its various information and record-keeping responsibilities, most systems have features that can provide important data to managers to aid them in decision making.

One of the keys to effective utilization of computers relates to the selectivity and depth of information stored in them. In installing a new computer system or modifying an existing one, what information to store in it is perhaps the most important decision. Beyond meeting the needs of human resources, a human resources computer system can also serve the rest of the organization and its managers. Managers should have some say in the design of the system or at the very least be familiar with its capabilities.

Some of the standard information contained in most human resources computer systems that is of value to managers includes demographic data about applicants, candidates, and employees, which is useful in developing recruitment plans. With their knowledge of possible sources of applicants, managers can assist human resources in its recruitment effort.

Employee turnover rates, which are helpful to managers in assessing their human resources needs, may also be stored. Perhaps more important, however, is information on how turnover rates and termination reasons compare with those of the total organization, making it possible to assess why employees are leaving a particular manager's unit.

Skills inventories provide managers with a readily accessible means of retrieving information about their employees' education, training, skills, and abilities. Such data is useful in personnel planning, in considering employees for promotion, and in evaluating the need for additional training. Performance-assessment reports offer managers a summary of performance levels within their organizational unit and show how those statistics compare with performance levels for the total organization. It is not that performance-assessment ratings must be uniform throughout the organization, rather that the reasons for variances in performance be identified.

Profiles on individual employees provide management with a summary of the information contained in employees' records. This data would include education, training, special skills, previous jobs—both within the organization and prior to joining the organization—salary history, benefits participation, and personal data. Profiles offer managers a ready reference for current information on employees as an alternative to maintaining separate files within the organizational unit.

Attendance and lateness records can also be stored. Computers have proved to be a particularly valuable tool in attendance-control programs. Some human resources information systems are tied into payroll-processing systems and can provide managers with the information pertaining to employees' absence and lateness for use in evaluating patterns of absenteeism and lateness, reasons for such, and other generalizations on attendance.

Much of the record keeping still performed by some managers, such as vacation and sick pay accrual, can be more easily and economically done by computers. Arbitration histories, helpful in saving time and money in preparing for arbitration cases, can be stored. Appropriate information regarding the organization's previous arbitration cases and their outcomes can be retrieved and organizations can evaluate the probability of winning current cases and make a determination on whether to proceed or settle.

Infractions of the organization's disciplinary policy, along with any disciplinary action taken, can be made available, as can records and statistics on past procedures to resolve employee concerns and problems, including the number of grievances, reasons, and how resolved.

Computers have numerous additional applications including the maintenance of seniority records, work-accident and injury reports, insurance and other benefits claims, and unemployment compensation statistics, to name a few. Through coordinated effort, human resources and managers can identify these additional needs for information and application of the computer to assist managers. Generally, most computer programs afford considerable flexibility in terms of what information can be supplied and in what configuration.

8

Working with the Human Resources Function to Resolve Employee Behavior Issues

We have emphasized how the human resources function can help managers carry out their responsibilities and avoid employee-related problems as they do so. This chapter will focus on how to resolve employee behavior problems when they do occur and utilize the human resources function to accomplish this goal. Employee-related problems do not always call for a reaction from management. Basically, people want to behave in an acceptable fashion, and when, on occasion, they do misbehave, they usually voluntarily change their behavior to conform to what is expected, without pressure from others. Sometimes, however, people cannot or will not behave properly, and in such cases others must initiate corrective action. In organizations, this responsibility is shouldered primarily by those in managerial positions.

There is no doubt that employees' attitudes, values, perceptions, and expectations have changed over recent decades and will continue to do so. Our purpose is not to pass judgment on these changes, but rather to broaden the reader's understanding of employees' behavior and how to influence it in a positive manner.

Employees' changing values often clash with more traditional organizational values and patterns of operating. This conflict is often the basis of employee behavior problems. To varying degrees, employees take job-related problems home and vice versa—their lives on the job and off the job are not mutually exclusive. Because societal and employee expectations of organizations have changed so much, employers, whether they like it or not, are virtually compelled to help employees who are in trouble, even if the trouble is not job-related. As we have noted, responsibility to employees can work for the benefit of both employers and employees.

In an attempt to maintain balance, people continuously strive to preserve a state of dynamic equilibrium. Because life is full of unknowns and is often stressful, people are easily physically or mentally thrown off balance. No matter what the cause, they usually behave in ways to gain and retain balance. A person's behavior in attempting to do this can be viewed as either productive or counterproductive.

When management perceives that an employee's behavior is counterproductive and the employee cannot or will not correct it independently, then management must initiate corrective action. Human resources should play a key role in providing support service to managers and employees in the corrective-action process. Action by management must be both offensive and defensive, and its first objective should be to help the employee change his or her own behavior. Given that employees are an organization's most valuable resource, then reasonable attempts to save that resource should be made before taking any steps to sever the relationship. Only in extremely unusual cases should this principle be violated. It is common for employees at any organizational level, and whether union or nonunion, to react defensively and to challenge any action by management that is seen as threatening to their welfare.

All too frequently, decisions by employers affecting employee job status have been rescinded because reviewing parties both internal and external to the organization have not been sufficiently convinced that management's actions were appropriate. Today, as never before, managers are being called on by all levels of government and by judges, juries, and arbitrators to substantiate their actions.

The Behavior Process

All behavior can be viewed as a conscious or subconscious attempt to increase, maintain, or avoid the loss of some level of need satisfaction. A person's "motivation" or "drive" is the observed behavior of striving to satisfy a need or needs. Although people share a common, broad range of needs, identifying the specific need causing a particular form of behavior and determining how and why a person's behavior is directed toward satisfaction of that need is difficult. To be effective, however, managers must develop an understanding of the motivational process.

No two people are exactly alike. They may share many traits and characteristics and yet be very different. General needs of people can be identified and categorized as physical, psychological, or both. They do not exist in any predetermined hierarchy, and their intensity and importance can change gradually or in an instant.

For example, people need food to sustain themselves. Can we conclude that eating is only a physical need? Do people eat to live or live to eat? The psychological significance of eating a particular food, say, or particular meal often far outweighs the physical need. At times people eat when they are not actually hungry and eat more than they need for physical sustenance. In the American culture, Thanksgiving with its traditional turkey and trimmings is a holiday in which eating has been ritualized and is highly symbolic. The food's preparation and the eating and posteating phases satisfy both physical and psychological needs.

We have outlined some broad human needs. They are not categorized as either physical or psychological because as we have seen, circumstances, conditions, perceptions, and values all interplay to make a rigidly structured classification impossible. People have needs for achievement, recognition, acceptance, power, self-respect, respect from others, justice, security, opportunity, sexual gratification, peace of mind, and freedom for self-expression. The list is endless.

To repeat, sorting out and identifying the needs that stimulate behavior or the motivational process is a difficult task. Behavior is shaped by a variety of factors. First, people are not born with the same attributes and abilities. To a substantial degree, a person's inherited traits directly and indirectly influence behavior. In addition, no two people experience the same environmental influences in life. So, behavior is in part inherited and in part shaped by the environment. When people work in an organization, they bring all of their inherited and learned patterns of behavior with them to the job. People are creatures of habit and tend to repeat behaviors that are rewarding to them in some manner, whether consciously or subconsciously. It is important for managers to recognize that employees' behavior patterns are well established before they begin careers in organizations. The extent to which managers can change employees' behavior is limited by the behavior-modification tools and techniques available for use by management, as well as the restrictions of the law, management's knowledge of techniques and the application of the tools, the degree of flexibility allowable in decision making, and other factors.

How often have we heard someone say he or she "is not motivated"? Whenever we observe behavior, however, we are seeing the motivational process in action. Motivation is the action part of the needs-satisfaction cycle. The conscious or subconscious needs people have at a given moment will cause behavior, if some sort of action, activity, or reaction can be associated with what is seen as eventual satisfaction of the needs.

Behavior can be logical and rational. It can also be illogical and irrational. Furthermore, interpretation of behavior is often colored by perceptual distortions and incomplete information. The effect is that, if attempts to analyze behavior are based on what is rational or logical, the wrong conclusions can easily be drawn. It is our belief, however, that one consistent element in human behavior is people's motivation to behave in ways that they perceive will ultimately satisfy their self-interests. If behavior is ultimately self-serving, then it can be said that employees do not work for their employers, they work for themselves. Their jobs and the organizations they work for are vehicles through which goals are achieved in order to satisfy needs.

The Meaning of Work to Employees

The importance of work-related activities varies among people and can change over time. Work activities must compete with other interests as a means of directly or indirectly satisfying employees' needs. The commitment employees are willing to make to their jobs is a function of expectations and the relative value of rewards of work as compared to costs. Rewards are defined as anything an employee views as a benefit to his or her welfare. Costs are defined as anything an employee views as a detriment.

Membership in any organization, whether voluntary or compulsory, generally involves some cost to the individual, including loss of freedom and individuality. When people join an organization, they have expectations of rewards from membership. When the expected rewards from work are fewer or less important than the perceived costs, dissatisfaction can show itself in numerous ways. The desired rewards are not only a function of expectations present at the time of hiring, but are also affected by changes the employee perceives in the costs associated with continued employment. We could formulate a rule of human behavior that says, the higher the costs, the higher the expected rewards. A corollary is that if the rewards are not attainable in the short term, expectations are likely to increase proportionally with the passage of time.

Organizations' reasons for employing and retaining employees are also self-serving. The work relationship is a process of mutual exchange. Organizations, through their managers, expect employees to make a commitment to achieving productivity goals that meld with the organization's overall goal of survival. If an organization is to continue to retain an employee, it expects the employee's contributions to be greater than the costs of his or her maintenance. On the other hand, if organizations expect employees to maintain membership and to make a strong commitment to work, then managers must maintain an environment where employees feel that rewards exceed costs. This is no easy task, considering the high expectations of many employees and the economic difficulties plaguing some industries.

As members of a pluralistic society, people belong to various organizations. Some memberships are voluntary whereas others are somewhat involuntary. Generally speaking, work in industrial, commercial, or service organizations is voluntary. No employee can be forced to maintain employment. But although employees are free to resign at any time, they may still feel trapped in their jobs. While they always have the option of quitting, it is often not feasible or realistic for them to do so. Economic conditions, age, family considerations, whether the employee has children in school, feeling about remaining in the community, and other important factors make membership in organizations for some employees more compulsory than voluntary. As long as employees feel compelled to maintain membership, they will do so. However, if employees feel locked in to their jobs and the perceived rewards are fewer than the costs, they will behave in ways to change the relationship of rewards to costs.

For some employees their jobs are strictly a means to other ends, while for others their jobs are an end in themselves. People in these two categories want different rewards from working. To the extent possible, reward systems should be flexible enough to satisfy differing employee needs. However, organizations are limited in what they can offer to employees, and employees' needs also change. Matching employees to jobs, cross-training, and flexible job-transfer and bidding programs are important. Additionally, employee wants may in some ways be insatiable.

The employee who derives considerable satisfaction from activities outside the job will often place less emphasis on job-related satisfaction of needs. These employees are not necessarily poor performers. If they are placed in jobs that require nothing more than a 9 to 5 commitment, then they may be quite satisfied and give a fair day's work for a fair day's pay. Conversely, employees who look for a high degree of challenge, opportunity for upward mobility, considerable recognition, and other, more deeply rooted expectations, will, if placed in jobs where such rewards are available and are distributed equitably, derive a great deal of job satisfaction and perform at a high level. In either case, if employees are not properly matched to jobs, problems can and will occur.

The challenge facing management is to provide sufficient rewards and satisfactions for employees to be attracted to and maintain employment while performing at required or expected levels. Rewards must be given on the basis of merit to reinforce positive behavior and good results. Some of the rewards that can be given for job performance are shown in Figure 9.

The Causes of Employee Behavior Problems

Life in today's society is both stressful and complex, and more and more, people are unable to cope effectively at times. High rates of inflation coupled with economic downturns cause even greater stress and strain because of the anxiety produced by uncertainty. Growing rates of violent crime, divorce, alcoholism and other forms of drug abuse, suicide, and mental and physical illnesss are in part related to rising inflation.

People vary in their ability to cope with stress. Under stress, a

Figure 9. Rewards or benefits from working in an organization.

Money—paycheck.
Money—benefits package.
Security—steady employment.
Pleasant work environment.
Safe work environment.
Interesting work.
Challenging work.
Recognition for performance (nonfinancial awards).
Competition.
Sense of pride in job or organizational affiliation.
Sense of accomplishment.
Contribution to the welfare of others.
Chance to earn status symbols.
Prestige of position or job title.
Opportunity to learn a skill.
Opportunity to participate in decision making.
Preferred work assignments.
Use of company equipment.
Discounts on company products or services.
Preference on overtime assignments.
Time off without penalty.
Discounts on used company equipment.
Opportunities to earn bonus awards.
Opportunities to get additional training on company time
    at company expense.
Flexible work schedule.
Compensatory time selection.
Site visits or field trips.
Preference on office location and decoration.
Sabbatical leave with pay.
Participation by invitation in special, sponsored-paid activities.
Freedom to choose special work assignments.
Paid memberships in professional organizations or societies.
Paid subscriptions to professional publications.
Reserved parking space.

person will eventually move toward either creative or destructive solutions. It is movement toward destructive solutions that is most likely to cause job-performance problems. Proactive managers recognize when problems are likely to occur and take preventative actions. Reactive managers wait until the damage has already been done.

In the job environment, four major sources that create disciplinary situations can be identified. They are: the kind of people hired, the nature of the work, the job environment, and the philosophy and operational practices of management. First, no matter how refined the selection process is, some people who should not have been hired will be. Second, not all jobs are good jobs, so for some types of work it is difficult to attract or retain good people. Third, work environments vary considerably both in terms of physical conditions and psychological climate. Hot, dirty, dangerous, and demanding work environments create considerable stress for employees, as do intensely competitive, cutthroat work climates. Under such physically or psychologically adverse conditions, the likelihood of employee behavior and performance problems increases. Last, the way an organization or a particular unit is managed significantly affects the ways in which employees behave.

A badly managed organization will experience employee behavior problems more frequently than a well-managed organization. This is especially true when poor supervision exists. A badly managed organization or unit may be one where supervisors and/or higher-level managers are arbitrary and dictatorial or one where inconsistency and permissiveness prevail. If employee misbehavior is tolerated and employees derive certain satisfactions from their misbehavior, frequently the behavior will be repeated. This is the case whether the situation is one of poor performance, excessive absence or lateness, or anything else.

Management has a responsibility to establish and consistently maintain standards and expectations for job performance. Consistency does not mean that all employees must or should be treated alike. It does mean that when facts, circumstances, records of service, and other significant factors are very similar, two employees, even though they may be in different organizational units, should receive the same treatment, assuming that the employees are working under the same organizational policies and in similar work environments.

Correcting Employee Misbehavior

Most employees who experience problems on the job, whether the cause is job- or non-job-related, are able to change on their own and avoid having management resort to serious disciplinary action. However, if behavior does have to be corrected and the best solutions are sought, cause and motivation for employee misbehavior should be identified. This, unfortunately, does not always seem possible or worth the effort, and in such cases, solutions are often directed merely at symptoms. This approach to problem solving is a hit-and-miss one that can bring about unintended side effects.

In addition, because of concerns about lawsuits, intervention by government agencies and possible arbitration, fear of no support from higher levels of management, and even fear of physical harm, many managers, particularly supervisors, avoid rather than address employee behavior problems. An attitude of apathy and indifference among managers is often adopted. This condition is dangerous and produces serious adverse consequences.

The majority of employees are as a rule willing to comply voluntarily with reasonable standards of conduct that are fairly administered. Usually, they expect management to set the proper examples for behavior and take action to correct employees who misbehave. Employees who are allowed to continue their misbehavior may influence others who may be tempted to misbehave and then see that they, too, can get away with it. Finally, employees who live up to their responsibilities lose respect for management when they see others getting away with misbehavior.

In correcting employee misbehavior, either a positive or a negative approach can be taken. Traditionally, the negative, or punitive, approach has been the one favored and is still the most widely used. The positive approach is rehabilitative and emphasizes self-control as opposed to punishment.

Under the punitive approach, employees learn to respond out of fear. Fear is a significant and effective influencer of behavior.

However, as fear diminishes, so does its effectiveness. Under this approach, employees usually learn to avoid getting caught or, when caught, look for ways to retaliate. The negative approach emphasizes oral and written warnings, suspensions from work, and assignment to undesirable jobs and work schedules.

Use of the positive, or rehabilitative, approach requires more patience and skill. But in the long term it often produces desired results, namely, a positive change in an employee's behavior. The positive approach stresses the use of counseling, training, retraining, probation in lieu of suspension from work, reducing or removing barriers that inhibit performance, and emphasizing the need for individuals to take responsibility. Depending on how they are applied, transfer, demotion, denying privileges, withholding merit salary increases, ignoring the employee, and peer pressure can be either punitive or rehabilitative.

Because discipline is an area in which managers have little, if any, formal training and because of the adverse consequences that result when discipline is applied improperly, the human resources function can and should play a key role. As we have emphasized, human resources' role, in general, is one of support and not control. Assumption of control should occur only when management has continually demonstrated an inability or unwillingness to use discipline properly. In fact, more and more, managers are utilizing human resources to help manage employee behavior problems, particularly in large organizations. The major reason for this is that reversals of management's decisions by outsiders and accompanying awards for damages to aggrieved parties have been too frequent.

In approaching employee behavior problems, a number of key considerations emerge. We have already discussed the need to identify causes as opposed to symptoms and the need to emphasize rehabilitative, as opposed to punitive, approaches. It is also essential that management, the initiator of discipline, establish that just cause for corrective action exists and, given the relevant facts and circumstances, that the recommended action is appropriate.

Human Resources' Role in the Corrective-Action Process

Because of the sensitive nature of employee behavior issues, human resources should develop policies outlining required or expected standards of conduct. Rules, or what we prefer to identify as stated employee responsibilities, are necessary in all organizations. They establish the boundaries for what organizations consider to be acceptable behavior. Without defined boundaries, two problems will result. First, employees may cross a boundary unintentionally and then be subject to discipline. Employees cannot be expected to react positively when being disciplined for misbehavior they were not aware was considered unacceptable. Second, in the absence of written standards, managers will independently establish different acceptable limits for employee behavior, leading to indefensible discriminatory treatment of employees.

Human resources should also develop procedures for managers to use in all facets of the corrective-action process. Managers should be provided with "tests" to apply to determine if just cause for corrective action exists, and they should be instructed in methods and techniques for obtaining and evaluating information. Additional procedures and guidelines should cover (1) how to conduct a corrective-action interview and counsel employees, (2) how to maintain current and accurate records, (3) how to determine the appropriate type and degree of corrective action, and (4) if discharge is necessary, how to conduct a discharge meeting.

Because managers initiate corrective action, the burden for establishing just cause is primarily theirs. Employees who break rules must be forewarned of the possible consequences of continued misconduct. Exceptions to the necessity for forewarning are for such misbehavior as immoral conduct, fighting, falsification, coming to work under the influence of drugs or intoxicants, major theft, and gross insubordination. In such cases employees, by virtue of common sense, are expected to know that one violation is grounds for discharge.

Rules should be limited in number and reasonably related to maintainng an orderly, safe, and efficient environment for the conduct of the organization's business.

The following questions can also help in determining whether the employer's action will be viewed as justifiable:

• Was a fair and impartial investigation of the incident conducted in a timely manner? In some cases immediate action is required. In such cases the best course of action is to suspend the employee pending the outcome of the investigation.

• Did the investigation produce sufficient evidence or proof of guilt? The general rule is: The more serious the misconduct, the higher the degree of proof required to impose severe discipline. Misbehavior that seriously impairs the employee's chances for future employment requires evidence or proof of guilt that is beyond reasonable doubt.

• Have the rules been consistently applied? Management cannot enforce the rules on a selective or subjective basis.

• Has disciplinary action been applied on the basis of the merits of the case? Consideration must be given to the employee's record of service, precedents, and prevailing and past practices.

As children we learn not to snitch on others. This principle is continually reinforced throughout our lives. However, not tattling, that is, not volunteering damaging testimony against others, can conflict with such values as honesty and doing what is legal and moral. Employees are generally reluctant to offer testimony against one another. However, what others have seen or heard is often essential to the corrective-action process, especially when actions imposed are appealed. The following suggestions may prove helpful in obtaining and evaluating information.

- Obtain testimony as quickly as possible after an incident has occurred. Willingness to testify frequently diminishes over time.
- Make a record of the testimony. Have it witnessed and be certain that those who gave testimony know that a record is being made.
- Have witnesses explain what they saw or heard in their own words. Avoid leading questions.
- Question witnesses to the extent necessary to ensure that their views are not biased. In any appeals proceedings testimony of witnesses will be aggressively cross-examined.
- Maintain confidentiality of witnesses and their testimony until identification is necessary.

Conducting a corrective-action interview is a sensitive matter and difficult to do successfully. The supervisor or higher-level manager may be upset for a variety of reasons, and the employee is apt to be anxious and even angry. It is important to remember that in a corrective-action interview, future relations with the employee are on the line. These suggestions can help assure a positive outcome:

Carry out a fair and impartial investigation.

Review all of the guidelines for applying discipline in a flexible yet consistent manner.

Schedule the interview within five work days of the day of the disciplinary incident.

Do not predetermine the guilt of the employee or the action to be taken.

Anticipate the employee's behavior.

Be in control of your emotions.

State your case against the employee in a clear, direct manner.

Do not go off on tangents or diatribes.

State the specific problem in terms of desired performance and actual performance.

Tell the employee the specific changes you expect in behavior.

Give the employee an opportunity to present his or her version of the incident.

Avoid arguing or debating with the employee.

Do not allow the employee to talk about vague or unrelated issues.

If the employee presents information showing that you do not have all the correct or complete information, close the meeting and reinvestigate the matter.

If you are convinced that you have sufficient and accurate information to carry out discipline, determine the discipline to be imposed after the employee has finished. Communicate your decision to him or her.

Indicate your confidence in the employee's ability to change behavior.

If the employee becomes angry and abusive, maintain control and conclude the meeting in a professional manner.

Advise the employee of his or her rights of appeal if he or she is dissatisfied with your decision.

Counseling is an integral facet of the supervisor-employee relationship. Its use should not be limited to a corrective-action review. When counseling is used to help an employee avoid a problem, or if a behavior problem already exists, to correct it, the following guidelines should be followed:

Prepare for the meeting. Know what you are trying to accomplish and have an agenda.

Keep in mind that a basic objective of counseling is to aid the employee help himself or herself change behavior.

To the extent possible be relaxed and try to reduce any observed anxiety, apprehension, anger, or hostility the employee may exhibit.

Clearly state the problem in terms of desired behavior and actual behavior.

Allow the employee to express his or her feelings and opinions.

Explain the rationale behind what you expect or require from the employee.

Inform the employee of what specific changes in behavior are required and the time frame for making them.

Get a commitment from the employee to change behavior.

End the meeting on a positive note. Make a record of the discussion and results. Let the employee review the record, and provide a copy of it if requested.

Maintaining current and accurate information about employees is easy if the following guidelines are applied:

Standardized record-keeping procedures with appropriate forms should be developed.

Managers, particularly supervisors, should be trained in how to keep records.

Time must be set aside on a routine basis to maintain records.

Managers who fail to maintain current, accurate information about employees should be subject to corrective action themselves.

Employees should be offered a copy of any written corrective-action information that will be included in their personnel files.

In determining the specific kind of corrective action to apply—and how much—consider whether just cause for taking disciplinary action has been established, whether the employee has violated a major or a minor rule, and what range of disciplinary action can be taken. You must also take into account the employee's past disciplinary record—what is the pattern of misconduct, its frequency, and how serious has it been.

What is the employee's record of service: how long has he worked in the organization, what is his performance record as compared to standards, and what is his history of raises, promotions, and attendance? Also consider:

What changes in behavior have been demonstrated by the employee as a result of previously imposed disciplinary action?

What is the state of the employee's physical and mental health?

What are the organization's past practices in administering discipline?

What are the organization's present policies and practices?

Why did the employee engage in misconduct?

How have other employees with similar records or in similar circumstances been treated?

If discharge is being considered, can the employee be easily replaced?

What will be the reaction of other employees if this employee is discharged?

What extenuating or mitigating facts or events in the employee's job or personal life are affecting his or her behavior?

Is the case against the employee strong enough to weather a review by others, either internal or external to the organization?

If discharge is the appropriate course of action,

Reassess the employee's entire record to be certain that discharge is appropriate.

Gather all supporting documents such as performance reviews, warnings, counseling meeting notes, and attendance records.

Review the plan of action with higher-level management and human resources.

Prepare an outline for the meeting and anticipate the employee's behavior and the questions you are likely to be asked.

Consider having another member of management or someone from human resources present.

To ensure consistency in the treatment of employees while allowing flexibility for each situation to be decided on its particular merits, human resources should be kept informed about action being considered or already taken against an employee. Because human resources is the central depository for information about employees, it can best assess the degree of consistency that exists among different organizational units.

Human resources should always, directly or on a consulting basis, participate in corrective-action issues where discharge is being considered. Discharge is, in effect, capital punishment for the employee. Before such action is taken, the case should be thoroughly reviewed by people who are less emotionally involved in the situation than the immediate supervisors and higher-level managers.

In attempting to identify underlying causes for employee behavior problems, human resources can be used to analyze information about employees to determine if statistically significant relationships exist among such factors as background, type of work, work schedule, and supervision. In this way it may be possible to uncover underlying causes for behavior problems. This type of analysis is best accomplished if employees' personnel records are maintained in a computerized human resources information system.

Analysis of this kind has proved particularly useful in identifying employee absence and lateness patterns and their underlying causes. For example, employees' ages and marital status are often directly related to absence on Friday night and Saturday work shifts. Young, single employees look forward to Friday night and often are not motivated to work. Additionally, partying on Friday evening into the early morning hours on Saturday is not conducive to working on Saturday. Another example would be high absence of minority employees in a particular work unit or among those classified in certain jobs. Absence could be due to prejudiced supervision, the nature of the work, or a poor match of employees with their jobs. If an employee appears to be heading for trouble or is in trouble and has not positively responded to management's attempts to influence behavior, human resources can provide valuable assistance. All organizations should have some kind of troubled-employee assistance program. The small organization with limited staff expertise and budget should develop liaisons with community social services and mental health organizations. The large organization would be able to afford the luxury of staff specialists to work with community service agencies.

Managers should be trained in the basics of counseling and to recognize when an employee's problem is beyond their skill level. Employees should know and believe that their supervisors and the organization are committed to helping them manage problems and personal crises. They should also feel that they can talk about job-related or personal problems with their supervisors or with human resources personnel without fear that what is said will be held against them. Some employees are unable to discuss job or personal problems candidly with their supervisor or anyone else in management. They are generally receptive to talking to someone whom they perceive as neutral or on their side. If an employee's problem is serious, human resources, if it does not have the expertise on staff, can coordinate assistance for the employee with community services specialists. It has been our experience that employees who benefit from such assistance will demonstrate their gratitude in many positive ways.

Most managers, at some point in their education, have received training in how to reward employees. Most, however, have not been trained in how to use discipline effectively as a management tool. As a result, they use the traditional punitive approach, often with undesired results. Human resources, with or without the use of consultants specializing in this area, should provide comprehensive training in the theory of discipline and in the practical application of organizational policies, procedures, and guidelines to actual cases or those likely to be encountered.

Employees should have an appeals procedure available to them for seeking redress for treatment viewed as unfair. Disciplinary actions are the ones most likely to be appealed. Human resources can participate at various stages of the appeals process by giving objective evaluation of the merits of the employees' grievance. When management is in error, it should assume responsibility for the error. It should not be human resources' role to reverse the decisions of management. If human resources has that authority and has to exercise it frequently, the results could be negative, dividing management and human resouces. Employees' feelings about management's fairness would surely be adversely affected. The correct approach is for managers to be as fair as possible. When an action is appealed and subsequently found to be in error, the reasons for the error should be explained to the managers involved. They should reverse their own decisions. To accomplish this human resources personnel must use tact and diplomacy, and managers must listen with open minds. When, on occasion, management is unwilling to reverse its decision, human resources should have the authority to reverse decisions of lower-level managers, subject to approval by executive management. The degree of authority vested in human resources depends on executive-level management's perception of the human resources function and its leadership role.

9

Increasing Your Effectiveness
as a Manager

We began this book by commenting on the impact of change on organizations and the environments in which they operate and what this means to managers who are responsible for the direction of their organizations. More often than not, we cannot control change, but by becoming more aware of it, we can prepare for its impact on the organization, its people, and its way of doing business.

Thus an unwritten but major responsibility of managers is to remain attuned to the environment and ready to interpret the implications of events to the organizations. Modern times record many examples of managers' failure to fulfill this responsibility. Yet, if managers do not, who will? While the human resources function has grown as a source of assistance to the organization and in the scope of its responsibility, clearly it is a staff function. As such, it was not designed to perform managers' jobs but to assist them and the organization.

To keep up with what is going on, management needs to develop what can best be described as a radar system. In developing this kind of awareness, rarely is insufficient information the problem; rather, selectivity is. Information is abundant and readily accessible. In fact, we are inundated with it from all around—television, radio, newspapers, magazines, meetings, conversations—the list is endless. The task is one of becoming sensitive to the countless sources of information, developing a sense of their reliability, being selective about what applies to organizations, and knowing how to use it all advantageously.

This task is formidable. The concerns and events organizations and managers have to deal with are no longer circumscribed by narrow geographic or ideological boundaries. Principally because of rapid technological advances and political and sociological changes, the world has become smaller. What transpires in distant countries often affects organizations at home and the environments in which they operate. Not only has change been dramatic within recent decades, but it has often taken place within a compacted time frame, making it difficult for societies as well as organizations to adapt.

No longer can managers be impervious to the world outside; nor can they manage with a narrow perspective of that world. Today's managers must be well informed, flexible, and facilitators of change within their organizations.

We have attempted to make managers aware that outside forces impact on an organization's people, who—and we stress this once again—are its most important asset. Any organization is a microcosm of the larger environment in which it operates. An organization's human resources function primarily in that larger world and only secondarily in the organizational milieu. Managers' ability to influence employees, therefore, is limited. By the same token, managers cannot attempt to change their employees' behavior in a way that contradicts external influences without encountering problems. It is the wise manager, therefore, who understands change and external pressures and works within them to direct behavior in the organization.

Where Our Society Is Today

For managers, much can be learned from the events of the past 20 years, particularly to help prepare for the future. While that future cannot be predicted with great accuracy, it is still important for organizations and their managers to be alert to how changes may affect management practices. Reflection on recent changes can give clues to future trends.

In the early 1960s, our society entered a period of greater awareness of itself and the individual. Our collective value system, way of doing things, and sense of commitment were called into question. Soon, so it appeared, the modus operandi was to denigrate or destroy almost anything that represented the pre-1960 years. In the wake of that destruction, few alternatives were offered. What did emerge unequivocally, however, was an emphasis on the individual that did not represent altruism, but rather hedonism, or what has been appropriately termed "me-ism."

Formerly, people's sense of commitment had been externally directed, focusing on belonging to and supporting a society in which people depended on each other. Commitment now became mostly internally directed, with an obsessive concern with self. In such a movement, individuals pursued their personal need to acquire new freedoms and self-fulfillment at the expense of duty, self-denial, self-discipline, and commitment to the common good. With their newly formed ethic, people came to look upon getting more of everything as a basic right, rather than as something to be desired or hoped for.

Furthermore, they became bold, if not militant, in seeking their new-found rights. Government responded to the moral pressure by enacting a considerable amount of legislation on a wide range of issues, promising job opportunities, a clean environment, expanded social welfare programs, and other reforms. All of these laws were designed to ensure that people could get what they felt entitled to and to provide protection and redress when it was denied them.

The fact that the economy was prosperous played a key role in the movement. Generations raised in an atmosphere of affluence had never known want and deprivation and therefore assumed that a prosperous economy was a natural phenomenon that could easily support their demands. Until the mid-1970s there was little reason, from their viewpoint, to doubt the validity of this conclusion.

The dress, the music, the language, and the life-styles of that period were a flamboyant statement of individuals doing their own thing in pursuit of mystical self-fulfillment. Many of the best-selling books preached the gospel of "getting in touch," personal exploration, and self-actualization as a person's highest priority. In some respects, people were made to feel guilty or deficient if they failed to, or simply did not want to, pursue self-interest to the hilt, at the expense of others.

This movement created, in many instances, tremendous problems for organizations, which basically require self-sacrifice and a sense of commitment on the part of their members. Influenced by the prosperous economy, people regarded organizations, especially those that were profit oriented, as being able to respond to their demands for better salaries, benefits, working conditions, job opportunities, and working hours. After all, the government had done so. Why shouldn't organizations respond in a like manner? However, people failed to understand or ignored the economic and sociopsychological realities of organizational life. They frequently demanded more of organizations than they were willing to give in return.

While perhaps not caught unawares by the shift in people's attitudes and the resulting effects on the work ethic, managers by and large were both confused and frustrated by events. Unaccustomed to being challenged, they perceived what was happening as a threat and responded accordingly, with the result that lines of division were more clearly delineated between management and employees.

Employees, too, became frustrated. Nurtured by a culture that affirmed people in their desire to have nearly every wish granted, employees had difficulty understanding why organizations could not meet their demands. Consequently, as the militancy of employees' demands increased, so did their distrust of organizations and its management.

Eventually, the balance between duty to self and duty to society was lost. Self-fulfillment actually became self-indulgence. No system or society, in the long term, can sustain these attitudes and beliefs without serious, adverse economic and socio-psychological consequences.

Where Our Society Is Going

Our society is now experiencing a sorting-out phase. On the one hand, we are sifting through the vast array of new freedoms and evaluating what they mean and their actual benefit to our lives. Conversely, we are growing more and more aware that a troubled economy poses a real possibility of limiting these freedoms. To suggest a return to the pre-1960 era is foolhardy, and it is unfair to imply that all the changes that have occurred during the last 20 years are necessarily bad.

The fact that Americans are searching for an identity—who they are as individuals—is potentially healthy both to them and to society as a whole. People are much more aware of their individual talents and strengths and are less hesitant to seek outlets for them. These outlets must be provided in such a way that both the individual and society benefit.

While it is tempting but hazardous to make predictions, some trends are emerging that afford a glimpse of what the future may hold. One such trend seems to be a discarding of much of the superficiality, in favor of substance, in relationships, whether with people, beliefs, or ideas. People seem to be searching for more selective and meaningful bonds with others and their environment.

As a consequence, a new sense of commitment is being shaped, rooted in relationships of substance. This is not to imply that the concept of self-denial, emphasizing suppression of individual desires in favor of the collective goals of society, is being revived. This newer form of commitment is the outgrowth of an impulse toward being part of something larger, with the expectation that it will benefit both the individual and society. What is critical to understanding this trend is that people are far more discriminating in developing relationships than they were formerly.

One More Look at the Management Process

Management as a process, activity, and profession is not a twentieth century phenomenon as some writers would have us believe. Management is as old as the human species. An examination of the historical writings of philosophers, poets, playwrights, scholars, noblemen, and religious and military leaders confirms that management has been applied to human endeavors and relationships since the beginning of recorded time. Many of the principles and practices of management thought to be modern creations have their roots deep in the past.

Management touches every aspect of our lives. Discounting the vagaries of natural phenomena, it can be said that the success or failure of individuals and organizations can be directly tied to the way in which management is applied.

Organizations and individuals who have developed sound management philosophies and can properly apply them will experience more success over time as compared to those who have not done so. Life for organizations and individuals is filled with opportunities, challenges, and problems. Those who manage well will capitalize on opportunities, meet challenges head on, and avoid or overcome problems.

Successes and failures are a given in life. Success is ego enhancing and acts as a positive reinforcer of behavior. Failure is ego deflating and acts as a negative influencer of behavior. But to capitalize on opporuntities involves taking some chances and risking failure. Prudent organizations and indivuduals attempt to reduce the risk element by carefully gathering and analyzing relevant information. However, decisions are rarely made with total objectivity or on the basis of complete, current, and accurate information.

When failure occurs, the less capable will indulge in self-pity and other negative feelings. The more capable will experience guilt, rejection, or depression as well, but will work through these feelings, become stronger, move forward, and learn to avoid repeating the same mistakes. The best managers respond in this way.

No one would deny that the cooperation of people is an integral part of any formula for organizational success and survival. As leaders, managers, within the limits of their authority, must build the framework and set the direction for cooperation among employees.

As we have said, often mere lip service is given to the idea that employees are an organization's most valuable resource. While the value of each particular employee can vary, all employees are valuable; and by virtue of their own behavior employees can increase or decrease their value. The same can be said for the value of organizations to employees. The employment relationship is one of mutual exchange and benefit. If it is to work properly, trust, responsibility, and commitment must come from both parties, management and employees.

It is important that both understand one another's needs, feelings, and concerns. In any relationship junctures are reached, often associated with problems. Such turning points often cause some emotional space between managers and employees. At this point, relationships either deteriorate or both parties strike a bargain to resolve the problem and work toward a better relationship. Commitment on the part of employers and employees means working through the difficult times as well as the good times.

Leadership Is the Key

The people of this nation in a scant 200 years have built the largest, most complex, productive, and affluent society that has ever existed on this planet. During the past 15 to 20 years, U.S. dominance in world markets has diminished. While in many industries the United States is still the world leader, in others its position has eroded significantly. The U.S. economic system is in a period of transition. We will either emerge a stronger nation or continue to fall behind our competitors. Our economic system and way of life are tied to capitalism. A viable, productive, and profitable economic system based on capitalism will ensure the continuance of our way of life and the social services provided by government.

For too long, managers have basked in the light of success, which in some industries and organizations has become merely a faint glow. Success and affluence too often breed complacency. The disease of complacency, if it becomes virulent, is difficult to cure. Too often the only cure is failure.

In recent years managers have sought scapegoats for the problems they are facing. Government, foreign competition, unions, and even employees have all come under the gun. We feel that all of these are, in part, the causes of problems. As stated at the outset, we live in a changing world. What has happened in business is that managers have failed to adapt to the changing environment.

Rather than continuing to project the blame onto others, it is time for managers to look at themselves and objectively assess their situation. One would hope that objectivity could lead to the development and implementation of plans for corrective action.

We see evidence that many managers are already moving in this direction and are cautiously optimistic about the future. For those managers who are indulging in denial and negativism, the following causes of problems are offered:

- Failure of management to invest sufficient money in research, new equipment, technology, and the training of employees.
- Rewards, including promotions, given on the basis of criteria other than job performance.
- Failure of management to develop attitudes and support systems to more effectively utilize employees.
- Acceptance of mediocrity in all aspects of organizational measures of performance.

Competent leadership at the top of any organization is essential for success. Leaders at the top set the tone and pace for all activities, and even in very large organizations the philosophy at the top will permeate downward. For this reason alone, only the most capable people should be allowed the privilege of occupying executive-level positions.

Economic turbulence began in the 1970s, and significant improvement is not expected even by the mid-1980s. This period will be one in which survival of the fittest is the rule. In more stable times, mistakes, even serious ones, could be made and recovered from before proving fatal. In the 1980s, this will not be the case, particularly in industries where profits are depressed and competition is intense. The right decisions at the right time and the fullest possible cooperation from employees to effectively carry out decisions will be essential.

In our opinion, management's role, especially that of executive-level management, is so important that job tenure should be based on performance, not on loyalty and seniority. Security is important, and too little can cause as many problems as too much. Most organizations, however, provide too much job security for managers and tolerate mismanagement and its consequences far too long before taking corrective action. It must be remembered that too much security breeds complacency. Complacency, as we have pointed out, is counterproductive.

The Consequences of Failure to Act

When employees perceive that they are being treated unfairly, they can and do find unlimited ways to protect themselves. Excessive absenteeism, abuse of privileges, increased turnover, deterioration in quality of output, unionization, and lawsuits are costly and impact adversely on profits. Time, money, and energy that could be better spent elsewhere will have to be directed toward containing and controlling problems.

As we have stated before, management is a physically and emotionally demanding profession. Serious problems with employees add additional stress. Excessive stress eventually takes a toll on people. Depression, drug abuse, serious mental illnesses, and physiological decay will occur more frequently. Some managers will recognize the danger signals before problems develop and may choose to leave management rather than attempt to cope with the stress. The payback period for the investment made by organizations in training and developing managers is long term. If managers leave the profession prematurely, the investment is not fully capitalized.

Organizations gain many advantages through emphasizing internal development of management talent. However, if employees perceive that the stresses and strains of managing are not worth the rewards of the job, they will not seek advancement into management positions. The long-term effect will be a deterioration in the overall quality of management.

In the long run, society in general will suffer, because mismanaged organizations eventually consume more than they provide. As a result, government receives less revenue from taxes, and social programs suffer. Scarcity will cause social tensions to increase, and sharper contrasts and divisions will separate society's "haves" and "have nots." Continued divisiveness can only lead to eventual social decay, and then everyone will lose.

We close this chapter and this book on a positive note, for it is not our intent to be the harbingers of doom. Our theme throughout has been the value of employees and of utilizing the human resources function to gain their trust and cooperation. We believe that organizations, with support from management, human resources, and employees, can alter the scenario outlined in this section and help restore prosperity to America.

Index